What Makes Switzerland Tick?

What Makes Switzerland Tick?

Richard Wildblood

The Book Guild Ltd.

Sussex, England

The Book Guild Ltd.
25 High Street,
Lewes, Sussex.

First published 1988
Reprinted 1992
© Richard Wildblood 1988
Set in Palacio
Photosetting by Oliver Dawkins Ltd,
Burgess Hill, Sussex.
Printed in Great Britain by
Antony Rowe Ltd.,
Chippenham, Wiltshire.

ISBN 0 86332 337 5

CONTENTS

FOREWORD

by
THE BRITISH AMBASSADOR TO SWITZERLAND,
MR J.R. RICH, C.M.G.

Richard Wildblood is to be congratulated on filling a real need – a brief, clear and accurate introduction to the constitutional, political, economic and social structures of a unique country. He gives an insight into the historical background over 700 years which has shaped the Swiss Confederation as it is today, together with a perceptive analysis of the attitudes of ordinary people and the way in which they participate in the governing of their country.

I commend his book warmly to the general reader. But it will also be of particular value to the business traveller or the holiday-maker who wishes to know more of what lies behind the surface of the beautiful and prosperous country which he visits either for professional purposes or for recreation. And it will serve as a valuable general introduction to the serious student who wishes to delve more deeply into one or other aspect of Swiss life and Swiss culture.

John Rich

8

ACKNOWLEDGEMENT

In compiling this booklet the writer has read the following books and wishes to thank their authors for the information which they contain:

Erich A. Kägi   'Demokratie Durchleuchtet'
                 'Wie hoch ist der Eintrittspreis?'

Hans Tschäni   'Profil der Schweiz'
                 'Wer regiert die Schweiz?'
                 'Wem gehört die Schweiz?'
                 'Parteien, Programme, Parolen'

Erich Grüner   'Politische Führungsgruppen im Bundesstaat'
                 'Die Parteien in der Schweiz'

Beat Junker and
Martin Fenner 'Bürger, Staat und Politik in der Schweiz'

Dieter Fahrni   'Schweizer Geschichte'

René Levy   'Die Schweizerische Sozialstruktur'

Paul Keller   'Die Schweiz warum?'

Oswald Sigg   'Die Politischen Institutionen der Schweiz'

Schweizer Brevier 1987

The writer is also grateful for the information given by the Bundesamt für Statistik in Bern.

He also wishes to thank most sincerely the British Ambassador to Switzerland, Mr J.R. Rich, C.M.G., for his extreme kindness in writing a foreword to this booklet.

He would also thank his good friends Hans Bless, John Ferguson Smith, and Jim and Marianne Homewood for the criticism and advice they have offered him, and Peter Hofmann and Peter Fehr for their kindness in gleaning information and reading the script

EXPLANATION OF SWISS INSTITUTIONS

THE SWISS CONFEDERATION is a federation of twenty-six individual states called cantons (six of which rank as half-cantons). These, in turn, are divided up into around 3,020 local authorities called communes.

THE SWISS FEDERAL PARLIAMENT consists of:

THE NATIONAL COUNCIL
(Representing the People)

THE STATES COUNCIL
(Representing the Cantons)

Together these form the FEDERAL ASSEMBLY

THE FEDERAL COUNCIL – the Cabinet or Government consisting of seven ministers elected by the Federal Assembly.

THE FEDERAL SUPREME COURT – the Judiciary situated in Lausanne.

THE FEDERAL INSURANCE COURT – deals with social security differences and is situated in Lucerne.

THE FEDERAL CHANCELLERY – the Cabinet Office.

THE SWISS NATIONAL BANK – a special statutory public limited company which controls the Swiss banking system.

SUVA – the Swiss Accident Insurance Association.

AHV – Insurance against Old Age and Bereavement (Widows and Orphans).

UV – Accident Insurance.

IV – Disablement Insurance.

AV – Unemployment Insurance.

EO – Indemnity for loss of earnings for militia men and civil defence recruits on being called up.

BV – Occupational Provision for Old Age, Disablement and Bereavement (Widows and Orphans) – supplementary to AHV.

VERNEHMLASSUNG (General Hearing) – this is the opportunity given to interest groups, cantons and the political parties to offer criticism, comment and suggestions for the improvement of a parliamentary measure at an early stage in the legislative process.

REFERENDUM – a general vote by the People.

INITIATIVE – the political means whereby the People initiate legislation.

The fact that certain titles and terms in this book are given in German and not in the other languages spoken in Switzerland is no reflection upon the latter, but simply because the writer is more conversant with German. All these titles and terms, of course, have their equivalent in the other languages.

INTRODUCTION

Whenever Switzerland is mentioned in conversation by people abroad the image given is invariably that of a small highly prosperous country in the heart of Europe, a home of banking, insurance and watch-making and in winter a paradise for skiers: and so it is and much more. With one of the highest standards of living in the world, full employment (unemployment rate in July 1986, 0.7 per cent) a modest indigenous crime rate, fairly low taxation and social harmony, it is unquestionably an extremely prosperous and peaceful nation. When, however, it is pointed out that it has not always been thus, that prosperity is a comparatively recent phenomenon in Switzerland, then people shake their heads incredulously, and if it is added that a hundred years ago Switzerland was one of Europe's poorer nations, with starvation still a possibility, the reaction is usually one of complete disbelief.

Yet the fact remains that for centuries the majority of Swiss people were poor. Switzerland has very few natural resources, and as she was heavily dependent on agriculture and the land was sparse, for many centuries she had the utmost difficulty in feeding her population. A hundred years ago half the population worked in agriculture, but only three quarters of the land is productive, and to make matters worse almost a third of the arable land lies in the mountainous areas. So that even until comparatively recently the Swiss could only make both ends meet by sending their sons abroad, originally as mercenaries into foreign armies and later as emigrants to the more prosperous parts of the earth. In the nineteenth century emigration was subsidized by the authorities.

The transformation that has occurred in Switzerland since the Second World War compares very favourably with the much-vaunted 'economic miracles' of West Germany and Japan, but less is known of it abroad. It did not happen purely by chance: much of Switzerland's success can be attributed to hard work, commonsense and foresight, but nevertheless geographical and historical factors did play a part in the development of the country, as will be shown in the story that follows.

ORIGINS

The original Swiss people who were in possession of the territory when the Romans invaded were principally two Celtic tribes, one called the Helvetii who inhabited the central part of present-day Switzerland and who gave their name to the country (Helvetia) and the other the Rhätii who lived in the eastern part of the country. After the defeat of the Helvetii at the hands of Julius Caesar at the Battle of Bibracte (58 BC), the territories of these Swiss tribes and Gaul became part of the Roman Empire.

1

Development

One determining factor in Switzerland's development has been her geographical position, namely the fact that she lies at the crossroads of Europe, at the junction of some of the most important trade routes running north-south and east-west. As has already been mentioned, Switzerland is a sparse country with few natural resources, and without these trade routes it would have been impossible for her to feed her people. What could not be produced at home to feed the population had to be procured from abroad by trading with the income derived from these trade routes. This also meant that from time immemorial Switzerland has been outward-looking, international in her outlook.

The trade routes across Switzerland would appear to have first come into prominence at the time of the Greeks and Etruscans, who bought their tin in Cornwall in southern England. The easiest way to procure the tin was to ship it to Greece via the Straits of Gibraltar and the Mediterranean. The Carthaginian fleet, however, had complete control of the western Mediterranean, and so the Greeks and their Etruscan merchants opted for the safer land routes through Europe, one of which ran along the Blenio valley, over the Lukmanier Pass to the rivers Rhine and Danube, and a second through Lombardy to the Aosta valley, over the Great St Bernard Pass to Martigny, from thence to the Lake of Neuchâtel and over the Jura to Châtillon-sur-Seine, down the Seine to Le Havre and across the Channel to Cornwall. For cash, the Swiss offered services and protection for the transit through Switzerland and prospered thereby. With the conquest of Carthage by the Romans in 146 BC, however, the Straits of Gibraltar became open again and the land routes over the Alps declined in importance.

This was of serious consequence for the Helvetii, and they

twice decided on mass-emigration to southern France, once in 107 BC and again in 58 BC. On both occasions they had to return home, the second time because they were heavily defeated by the Roman legions in Gaul at the Battle of Bibracte. They returned to find that their lands, in their absence, had themselves been conquered by the Romans. The Romans were hated as invaders, but this conquest did mean that the transit routes over the Alps regained their importance, and this proved to be an enormous blessing to the Helvetii. New roads were built across the Alps linking the territory with Rome, and a period of prosperity ensued which lasted for about three hundred years.

The power of the Roman Empire, however, gradually began to wane. In 260 AD a Germanic tribe, the Alemanni, penetrated the Limes, the Roman Empire's northern defences, drove the indigenous peoples into the mountain fastnesses and settled in the central part of present-day Switzerland. The Burgundians settled in the west of Switzerland and the Langobards in the south.

The fact that Switzerland has been formed from different origins is of significance because these original tribes either brought with them or developed different cultural backgrounds, and either spoke or adopted different languages. It was from this amalgam of tribes and indigenous peoples that modern Switzerland was to develop. The tribe which, perhaps, had the most influence on the development of the country were the Alemanni. They settled in the present German-speaking part of the country and brought with them a very strong love of freedom and independence and a highly developed sense of civic responsibility, for whilst they fully respected private property, they always had regard for the common weal by retaining a part of their land as common property to be reserved for common cultivation. Remnants of this co-operative form of cultivation still remain in the mountain-cantons in the form of 'Korporationen' (Co-operatives), 'Allmenden' (Common land) or 'Genossamen' (Village co-operatives). In these co-operatives decisions were taken collectively at public meetings, and it is here that we find the origin of the idea, in Switzerland, that the people are 'sovereign', that the people are the final arbitors in political and social matters and not, as was the case in many other countries, the emperor, monarch or ruler. The Alemanni also brought with them the desire for a self-elected legal system which has left its mark on the Swiss legal framework.

With the fall of the Roman Empire in the fifth century trade over the Swiss Alps was again very much reduced. All that was required was to meet the requirements of the princely houses and those of the Church.

In the sixth century the Burgundians and the Alemanni were conquered by the Franks, and when the empire of Charles the Great was divided up in 870, Burgundy was given to the West Franks and the Alemanni territories to the East Franks. The Franks spread the feudal system throughout Europe and with it the disposal of the land and its products and the people who tilled that land passed into the hands of a belligerent nobility. In recompense for the bequeathing of the land to them these noble landlords were required to do military service for their king and to administer their territories. As regards the peasants, the landowners had an obligation to protect them, but they also had the right to administer the law and to levy taxes.

This conception of feudalism with power in the hands of an emperor and large land-owning families, and with the peasants absolutely subject to them, was a far cry from the old Alemannic idea of small self-governing communities with power in the hands of the people. Two centuries of stagnation followed in which the land-owning families, bent on their own personal aggrandisement, fought each other and devastated the land, as a result of which, by the end of the thirteenth century the area of present-day German-speaking Switzerland and a large part of Swabia were in the control of the Habsburgs. During the tenth and eleventh centuries the peasants lived from hand to mouth, trade and industry deteriorated and the towns fell into decay. But the old Alemannic ideas of freedom and independence never fully died out, and when during the twelfth and thirteenth centuries agriculture took on a new lease of life, thanks to improved farming methods, the peasants began to rent their land and assert their independence once more. This was the period when new towns began to be founded again because the Muslims, who had invaded the Mediterranean basin during the seventh century, had now been driven back, and places such as Genoa and Venice had become important harbours and trading-centres. Trade routes from these two places to North Germany and Flanders led through Switzerland and trade on these transit routes revived once more. But with a difference: the trade route which from now on was to prove to be the most important led neither over the Great St Bernard Pass nor over the Lukmanier Pass, but over the St Gotthard Pass.

Just as in the towns guilds had become established whose desire it was to be free of their hereditary aristocratic rulers, so in the foothills of the Alps, valley communities had developed which were self-governing, and whose political and social decisions were taken at the Landsgemeinde (public assembly) in true Alemannic tradition. The Urner were one of these valley communities. They lived at the foot of the St Gotthard Pass and had traded with their mule-packs over the St Gotthard Pass for many years. Many had established themselves as highly reputable international traders, but it was not until 1240 that this trading-route took on a special significance, namely when the men of the Canton Uri succeeded in building a new bridge over the River Reuss in the wild Schöllenen ravine, and so made the route via the Reuss valley and the St Gotthard Pass the shortest connection between south and north.

During the next fifty years there was a massive increase in trade over this Pass, so much so that the men of the cantons around Lake Lucerne had to decide whether they would allow the revenue from the duties they levied on this transit-route to be poured into the coffers of the Holy Roman Empire, of which their territories formed part, or whether the time had not come to assert their independence and detach themselves from it. Influenced no doubt by the intense love of freedom derived from their Alemanni ancestors, and the tradition of independence that had since developed, they opted for the latter course and thereby laid the corner-stone of modern Switzerland.

Tradition has it that in the first days of August, 1291, men of the valley communities of Uri, Schwyz and Unterwalden met secretly and by night, in a remote meadow at Rütli on the shores of Lake Lucerne, swore to exclude the representatives of their feudal overlords from their territories, and pledged mutual assistance in the event of any of their members being attacked in consequence of the oath which they had given. This they not only swore but put in writing, in what is known as the Federal Letter which has been preserved to this day.

The reaction from the feudal overlords was not long in coming. They could not regard these events with indifference, firstly because the revenue to be derived from the St Gotthard trade-route was too great to be foregone, and secondly because it was inadmissible to have the old Alemannic conception of the 'sovereignty of the people' put into effect in the very heart of their territories.

The Habsburgs were determined to bring the pass fully under their control, and in order to accomplish this they sent an Austrian army to block it. For the Swiss Confederates it was a matter of economic and political life and death that it should remain in their hands, so they called in the help of Zurich by signing a first treaty with them and then took on the Austrian troops. Against all expectations the Confederates finally prevailed, the Austrian army was defeated at Morgarten in 1315, and within a few years the cantons of Lucerne, Zurich, Glarus, Zug and Bern had joined the Confederation, and again at the Battle of Sempach in 1386.

The northern access to the St Gotthard transit-route was now firmly in the hands of the Confederates, but the southern access was not. In order to secure this, the Urner and Obwaldner occupied the Levantina valley as far as Bellinzona in 1403.

The Confederates also extended their influence northwards as far as Basel and eastwards as far as Chur by concluding trade treaties, and after annexing Thurgau in 1460, they concluded an eternal peace treaty with Austria in 1474 and so secured their eastern frontier. The final fetters of the Holy Roman Empire were thrown off after the Battle of Dornach in 1499.

After the peace treaty with Austria in 1474, the Confederates turned their attention westwards to where the Duke of Burgundy, Charles the Bold, was excluding them from the French and Spanish markets. The Duke of Burgundy's armies were defeated by the Bernese at the Battles of Murten and Grandson in 1476, and the Duke himself died a year later. Bern now had the upper hand and her armies penetrated to the gates of Geneva. Finally, the Canton of Vaud was brought to submission in 1536 and made a vassal state. The way now lay open for trade with Geneva, Lyons, Spain and the newly-founded colonies overseas.

Meanwhile the Confederates had also turned their attention southwards again. Foolishly they embarked upon a war of aggrandisement into the Plain of Lombardy, and it was here that they encountered concentrated musketry-fire for the first time, at the hands of the French. They were so heavily defeated at the

Battle of Marignano in 1515 that they abandoned their policy of aggrandisement for ever, withdrew into their own territories and adopted a policy of neutrality. The boundaries of the Swiss Confederation now remained much the same for almost three hundred years.

The next three hundred years were years of turmoil for the Swiss Confederation. The Confederation was politically and economically largely dependent on financial arrangements with European princely houses, in which the latter bought the right to enlist mercenaries in Switzerland. This became a very lucrative business and created a powerful burgher plutocracy in the towns. The peasants resented this and periodically they revolted accordingly. In addition, this feud between the Swiss rural and urban areas was fuelled by religious discord.

Almost immediately after the Swiss were defeated at the Battle of Marignano and decided upon a policy of neutrality, Martin Luther pinned his ninety-five articles on the door of Wittenberg Cathedral: the Reformation had broken out, and it was to shake the Swiss Confederation to its very foundations. The country became a focal point of religious discord and many of the quarrels were only settled by force of arms. Basically, the centre of the country remained faithful to the Old Faith, but the towns and cities mostly adopted Protestantism. Yet despite the disintegrating effect which the Reformation had, it was not wholly harmful. In Geneva the Reformer Calvin legalized usury (the taking of interest on a loan) which the Roman Catholic Church had continually forbidden, and in so doing he laid the foundations of a future prosperous Swiss banking system. This was strengthened by an influx of religious refugees from France who had financial expertise. Providing that their acceptance would stimulate Swiss trade and industry, religious refugees were admitted into the country: the silk trade in Basel and Zurich was founded by refugees from Italy and the north. Refugees who had means were often excluded from the towns by the guilds and had to establish their businesses in rural areas. This dispersing of industry proved to be beneficial, and the Swiss textile and watch-making industries prospered, mainly as home industries. By the end of the eighteenth century Switzerland had become one of the most industrialized countries in Europe, but she remained a poorish country because she still could not produce enough food at home to feed her people. In 1817 thousands died of hunger, and it was not until the end of the nineteenth century that the spectre of starvation in Switzerland was finally banished. During the seventeenth and eighteenth centuries, however, the Old Confederation tended to stagnate politically. Added to the discontent caused by the trade in mercenaries were religious civil war and rivalries between the towns and surrounding rural areas, which also entailed bloodshed and devastation. Therefore, whilst over the centuries the cantons had managed to throw off the rigid authority of the hereditary powers, they still lacked the cohesion and willingness to co-operate which were necessary for the creation of a unified state: this would have to be provided from without. It came in the form of Napoleon who, with his Revolutionary armies, had little difficulty in occupying the country in 1798.

Out of a loose alliance of squabbling states Napoleon now welded together a unified country for the first time in what was known as the Helvetic Republic. In the cantons the battle was now joined between the conservative faction, the federalists who wished to retain sovereignty for the cantons and the unitarians who strove for a unified state. Such was the bitterness and strife which ensued that Napoleon intervened again in 1803. He revised the constitution of 1799 in the form of a compromise: it is called the 'Mediation'. It brought into the Swiss State the former vassal areas of Aargau, Thurgau, Ticino and Vaud and the former affiliated states of St Gallen and Graubünden. This second state structure lasted for ten years.

In the peace treaty drafted by the Congress of Vienna after Napoleon's defeat in 1815, the Old Confederation was restored, the aristocrats regained many of their privileges and certain civic rights were withdrawn. Geneva, the Valais and Neuchâtel were incorporated in the Swiss State, and Bern received the Jura as compensation for the loss of her vassal territories in the Aargau and Vaud.

The struggle between the conservative faction, the federalists, and the progressive faction, the unitarians, was by no means settled by the Congress of Vienna. The progressive ideas of the French Revolution which stemmed from the Enlightenment were still alive and began to flare up. Liberal movements began to revive strongly and the 'Regeneration' set in. The ideas of personal freedom and equality before the law began to fight their way through. In 1819 the Zofinger Student Movement took up the fight against the re-introduction of privilege. There was an ever-increasing demand on the part of the ordinary citizen for the abolition of the authority and privileges of the nobility and of the Church and for freely-elected parliaments which would legislate laws to establish the rights of the individual.

Trade was also restricted by economic impediments imposed by the corporations and guilds, and above all by tolls levied at town boundaries and on bridges. This stagnation was economic as well as political.

The new age of Liberalism could not be held back. In many cantons aristocratic privileges were withdrawn, and new cantonal constitutions drawn up which guaranteed voting and civic rights to the people. Both political and economic considerations demanded a unified state, but the Catholic cantons were determined to protect themselves. They met in Lucerne in 1845 and formed a military defence alliance called the Sonderbund. The progressives were appalled by this and reacted vehemently. In the Tagsatzung, the parliament of the Old Confederation, the Liberal-Radicals now had twelve full and two half votes out of the twenty-two seats, and so were in a position to commission General Dufour to suppress the uprising in Lucerne. After a short campaign he occupied the town, and the canton of Valais was the last member of the Sonderbund Alliance to surrender on 29 November 1847.

Liberalism had finally triumphed. The last Tagsatzung of the Old Confederation ratified a new constitution on 12 September 1848.

Save for the short duration of the Helvetic Republic, for 550 years the Old Confederation had been a loose alliance of small states: now, by ratifying the new constitution, the Swiss took the important step to becoming a federal state.

2

The Swiss Federal Constitution

It should be remembered that although Switzerland became a united country in 1848, it nevertheless remained a federation of sovereign states called cantons with their own constitutions and laws, but all now under one roof. While the Federal Constitution is accepted as being the highest authority in the land, it nevertheless recognizes the sovereignty of the cantons. Perhaps this hesitancy of outlook is best exemplified by the fact that whilst all Swiss citizens would immediately call themselves Swiss, there was great tardiness in finally adopting a national anthem. A balance must be kept between the Federal State and the cantons, and in order to maintain this equilibrium, a certain aloofness to the Federal State must be shown. The Federal Constitution is no exception to this, for whilst in certain areas it increased the power of the central authority in 1848, by allocating more commitments to it, it also recognized the sovereignty of the cantons, by assigning to them either sole responsibility or joint responsibility in a wide field of competencies.

In accordance with the Federal Constitution of 1848, the Federal Government must undertake to protect Switzerland from external attack, to preserve law and order within, and to uphold the basic rights of the citizen. The Federal Constitution of 1848 stipulates that the Legislature shall consist of two chambers, the National Council and the States Council, whose members shall be elected democratically by the people. The Executive shall be the Federal Council and shall consist of seven councillors to be elected by the joint houses of Parliament, which together form the Federal Assembly. The Federal Constitution also gave the right for 50,000 enfranchised citizens (men) to demand an obligatory referendum for the total revision of the Federal Constitution.

The Federal Constitution of 1848 was an obvious compromise

between the views of the conservative federalists and those of the progressive liberals. A concession to the federalists was the stipulation that the National Council and the States Council were to be of equal standing, and that in the States Council the full cantons should have two votes, irrespective of the size of the canton, and the half cantons one vote each.

As the government of the country was mainly in the hands of the Liberal-Radicals and as it was felt by many people that the democratic process had not been carried far enough, it was inevitable that democracy should proceed further. Several cantons experimented with new democratic forms and amended their constitutions, and eventually the Federal Constitution had to be revised in 1874 in order to incorporate the more successful results from these experiments.

In the revision of the Federal Constitution in 1874, the fundamentals of the 1848 Federal Constitution were retained, but the Facultative Referendum was also introduced. In 1891 the Constitutional or Peoples' Initiative was brought in: these will be explained in a later chapter. Later proportional representation to the National Council was adopted. Since then there have been many adjustments to the Federal Constitution culminating in the women's right to vote in 1971.

With the Federal Constitution of 1848 and its revision in 1874 and with the supplementation of the Peoples' Initiative in 1891, the tender sapling of a democratic state system which the Alemanni planted when they invaded Switzerland in the third century had now grown to full stature. It had survived the deep snows of the Dark Ages and the storms and tempests of Habsburg arbitrary rule: nor had it been stifled by the self-interest of the political rivalries of the towns and rural areas. In the next hundred years it was to yield fruit abundantly. What were the special conditions of the Swiss political soil and climate which made the crop so bountiful? We shall try to give an answer in the chapters that follow.

3

Federalism

The Federal State, the Cantons and Communes

The first essential feature which is conducive to Swiss political prosperity is federalism: it is one of the basic elements of the Swiss democratic political structure. One definition of a federation is 'a union of government in which several states, while independent in home affairs, combine for national and general purposes': such roughly is Switzerland, namely a federation of sovereign states called cantons.

When in 1848 the Swiss cantons came together to form the Swiss Confederation, they had been independent states for many years. In this act of union they merely strengthened their common ties and created a higher authority, without at the same time forfeiting their individual independence. The continued existence of the Swiss cantons is guaranteed by Swiss Federal law: the Federal State of its own volition can neither dissolve a canton nor create a new one: even a modification of cantonal boundaries requires the approval of all the people concerned.

Switzerland is divided up into twenty-six cantons (six of which rank as half cantons), and these are divided up again into around 3,020 local authorities called communes. The cantons are not merely administrative areas of a centralized state, but rather independent small states: they have their own constitutions, create their own authorities, elect their own governments, parliaments and administrative bodies. They also have their own law-courts. For the most part the Federal law only prescribes certain basic requirements of the cantons, namely a recognition of certain basic principles. The Federal State cannot impose a governor on a canton: it may only intervene in a canton, if the cantonal government requests it to do so to restore law and order, or if cantonal government has completely broken down.

It is the aim of federalism to leave as much decision making as possible to the cantons. Before the Federal Constitution was compiled in 1848, the cantons were already sovereign states with their own currency and revenue derived from taxes imposed at their frontiers and at bridges. In determining the Federal Constitution in 1848 and its revision in 1874, a balance had to be struck between the creation of an overall economic area which would allow trade to develop freely, and the preservation of individual cantonal characteristics. Over a period of time a division of competencies was worked out between the Federal State and the cantons. Certain competencies belong exclusively to the Federal State, and these are clearly laid down in the Federal Constitution: to these belong the preservation of peace, both external and internal, foreign affairs, the safeguarding of the cantonal institutions, legislation in respect of the civil and penal code and the law of obligation, the minting of money, the post and telegraph services, explosives, railways, shipping, air-transport, customs dues, military organization and the control of weights and measures, among others. All those competencies which are not expressly assigned to the Federal State in the Federal Constitution are the concern of the cantons. The cantons have their own revenue and determine their own taxes. They receive certain monies from the Federal authorities, but for most this represents only a small part of their income.

The cantons have extensive powers of legislation in certain fields, but in others they merely execute the laws enacted by the Federal State, such as those which come under the civil and penal code and the law of obligation. There is usually a right of appeal to the Federal Supreme Court against the findings of the cantonal courts.

The Federal State does have a certain influence over the cantons in that it can often offer incentives to them to perform certain tasks by promising them subsidies, but basically the cantons are financially very largely independent of the Federal State.

The cantons are not subject to any political control by the Federal State, but because there is a danger that independent action by a canton could harm the general good, a constitutional safeguard has been incorporated, in that cantonal constitutions must be sanctioned by the Federal Assembly, and also in that certain cantonal laws and decrees require the approval of the

Federal Council. The Federal Council, however, cannot reject a cantonal law on any grounds other than that it is unconstitutional.

The cantons participate as equal partners in the formulation and expression of the public will, and they have a say in the appointment of the organs of state. Each canton can submit a cantonal initiative direct to the Federal Assembly, and all have access to the Vernehmlassung (general hearing) whenever a new law is being drawn up. In certain instances the cantons must be consulted before a Federal decision is taken.

All cantons are of equal standing irrespective of size, except that in the States Council the half cantons have only one vote as against the full cantons two.

In view of the ever more complicated problems of political life, cantons often come together for some specific objective. Cantonal ministers of the same department meet together regularly to discuss common problems: this is especially true in the fields of education and finance. They also have close contacts with the Federal departmental chairmen.

In some cantons political rights are more far-reaching than those of the Federal State itself, because in certain cantons the enfranchised citizens are entitled to an extended use of initiative and referendum in cantonal affairs. All cantons have the referendum and initiative, but these vary in content and procedure from canton to canton.

Most cantons have an elected parliament, housed in a parliament building, but the old form of direct democracy still prevails in what are called the five 'Landsgemeinde' (public assembly) cantons: these are Obwalden, Nidwalden, Appenzell Ausserrhoden, Appenzell Innerrhoden and Glarus. Here cantonal business is transacted at an annual public gathering, held in the open air, on the last Sunday of April for the first four and on the first Sunday in May for Glarus. These traditional ceremonies are extremely colourful and date back to the early days of the Old Swiss Confederation. At these assemblies a president called a Landammann is elected, together with a government and judges, and it is here that the most important cantonal business is discussed and decided upon by direct vote.

In order to decentralize authority further and involve citizens more closely, the communes were also given a share in the allocation of tasks and duties. The communes vary tremendously in size, from small hamlets with less than 100 inhabitants to Zurich with more than 350,000.

The communes are mentioned in the Federal Constitution with reference to their shared responsibility in the conveying of civil rights and the right of domicile.

The commune is not merely the lowest organ of state administration: the communes also enjoy a certain amount of autonomy in that they have their own constitutions, governments and adminstration and they levy their own taxes. The principal duties of a commune authority will include the administration of commune finances, property and land, the supervision of social welfare, public services (gas, water and electricity), the fire-services and refuse-disposal etc. In addition, the communes fulfil many other duties as representatives of the canton and the Federal State.

The partnership between the Federal State, the cantons and the communes is effected by means of federalism. Federalism widely permeates Swiss political life, as we shall see when we consider the Swiss political institutions. It is so important to Switzerland, and could be of importance to other nations, that an assessment of its political value should be made. What are its advantages and disadvantages?

Perhaps the greatest disadvantage of federalism is that whereas a state with a centralized form of government can take decisions quickly, because this type of state appoints its own officials and directs their activities, in a federalistic state decision-making tends to be long drawn out. This may be because the competencies belonging to the Federal State and cantons are not clearly defined and time is needed to clarify them, or simply because there are more parties to be considered. A second criticism of a federalistic state is that conflicting decisions may lead to a lack of cohesion and thereby to confusion: a canton acting within its own competencies may frustrate the wishes of central authority and those of other cantons. In that the Swiss cantons are separate states which, in certain fields, interpret and administer Federal law independently and in other fields enact their own laws, this can lead to a difference in the execution of the law and thereby to inequalities between the cantons. A further criticism of federalism is that in its effort to protect minorities, it has a tendency towards over-representation, and thereby to an inequality of representation and political influence. In the States Council, for example, the full cantons have the same number of seats, irrespective of the size of the canton.

But against these disadvantages when compared with a centralized state federalism can offer many advantages. Firstly federalism helps to provide an answer to variety within a country. In all countries there are internal differences to a greater of lesser degree, and often there are minorities which form majorities in certain parts of the country. This is true of Switzerland, where taking the country as a whole the French-speaking population form a minority (twenty per cent), but in western Switzerland they constitute an overwhelming majority. Federalism gives the opportunity to such minorities to order their own affairs independently in certain areas, and this in its turn defuses tension. Secondly, federalism softens the application of national law, in that it acts as a shock-absorber against central authority. The application of federal law is softened, on the one hand, in that it is not administered by national state officials but by local magistrates who are known personally to the people, and on the other, because although there is a certain amount of supervision from above, the cantons themselves can often decide how a law shall be introduced. Federalism also has the advantage that it acts as a restraint on central authority: the political authority of the cantons restricts that of the Federal State.

The fact that Switzerland is composed of a number of cantons, each with its own political power and administrative organs, offers wide-spread opportunity for political experimentation. The proportional representation voting system, as well as the introduction of the women's right to vote, were first tried out at cantonal level before they were introduced at national level.

But perhaps the greatest advantage that the federalistic state has over the centralized state is that it identifies the individual more closely with political responsibility, and involves many more people in political affairs. In a centralized state political power is often so remote that there is a lack of political intimacy between the citizen and his rulers. In a centralized state, also, there is a tendency to regard people as objects and to stereotype them. The smaller the unit, the more personal it is possible to be.

If, however, the object of the political exercise is to involve as many people as possible as closely as possible in public affairs, then small units must be employed because firstly, the smaller the unit the easier it is to be comprehended, and secondly, the smaller the unit the more personal it is and the easier it is for the individual to become involved.

Switzerland, as has been pointed out, has developed from an amalgam of tribes which either brought with them or later developed different backgrounds: four different languages are spoken within the country, three different cultures from three different backgrounds in neighbouring countries are represented here, and the people confess largely to two different faiths. The disintegrating forces throughout Switzerland's history have been tremendous, and yet from all these disparate elements a state has been welded together. This is surely attributable, in no small part, to federalism. Could not Switzerland's experience be helpful to other countries with similar problems? Could not federalism, perhaps, be the answer to Europe's search for cohesion?

4

The Creation of the Canton of Jura

The proof that federalism has a potential for wider application is given by the creation of the new canton of Jura in 1978, when it became the official twenty-third canton of the Swiss Confederation. In order to understand the complexities of the Jura question it is necessary to know something of its historical background.

In the early Middle Ages this north-western part of Switzerland was ruled by the bishops of Basel, whose diocese also included parts of Alsace and southern Germany, as well as parts of the Jura region. In the year 1000 AD the Bishop of Basel was appointed a Prince of the Holy Roman Empire, and from that day onwards he and his successors strove to create a worldly power out of their spiritual domain.

Gradually they acquired certain surrounding territories in the southern Jura which today form part of Switzerland. Whilst all these territories came under one jurisdiction, namely the fief of the Bishop of Basel, they still retained sufficient independence to conclude individual treaties with their neighbours, and as the result of this they developed a divided loyalty to their overlord, the Bishop of Basel, and to their allies. This was especially true of the southern part of the Jura where the people came into close relationship with Bern and thereby with the Swiss Confederation: the northern part of the Jura, however, remained closer to the Holy Roman Empire. After the Reformation, as a result of religious differences, the divide between the two parts of the Jura became even more pronounced.

When Napoleon conquered this part of the world the two parts of the Jura were, for a time, incorporated in France, but at the Restoration in 1815, both parts were given to the German-speaking canton of Bern, despite the fact that the Jura region at that time was, for the most part, French-speaking. The northern part of the Jura had little in common with Bern, the people spoke a different language, most had a different religion and background, and their incorporation in the canton of Bern was widely regarded as an arbitrary act.

In religious matters there was continual friction between the northern Jura and Bern throughout the nineteenth century, and the situation was also aggravated by the fact that during this century many German-speaking immigrants came into the southern Jura from other parts of Switzerland.

A separation of the Jura region from Bern had already been mooted during the nineteenth century and also during the First World War, but it was only after the Second World War that the problem became acute. The flash-point came in 1947 when the Bern Cantonal Parliament refused to appoint a French-speaking councillor (he spoke no word of German) as head of the cantonal Department of Public Works.

The feelings of the French-speaking Jura people were inflamed by this refusal, and they started a movement to work towards better representation for the French-speaking people in the Jura area of the canton of Bern. This new movement developed into the 'rassemblement jurassien': it found its support mostly in the northern Jura. The people of the southern Jura were, for the most part, happy to remain in the canton of Bern: they formed themselves into the 'union des Patriotes jurassiens'. On both sides youth movements were also formed.

In 1950 the Canton of Bern Constitution was revised to allow the French-speaking Jurassians better political representation, but this was no longer enough to satisfy the Separatists, who began to call openly for a separation of the Jura region from the canton of Bern. In 1958 the Separatists demanded a referendum to allow the people of the Jura districts to vote on the issue. The request was heavily defeated at a plebiscite of all the people of Bern Canton, but in the Jura region itself the voting was almost equally divided: the northern part voted in favour of a referendum, but the southern part voted against such a referendum being held.

Feelings now ran very high. The Separatists became more and more frustrated and began to take direct action: the farms of German-speaking farmers were set on fire and dynamite was placed under railway lines. The suggestion that the solution to the problem lay in the creation of two half-cantons of the Jura area met with little approval. The situation was now extremely serious, but as had happened so often in previous Swiss history, the common sense and broad-mindedness of the Swiss people came to the rescue and federalism proferred the required solution.

It was at this point in 1968 that the Bernese Cantonal government showed great tolerance and foresight by setting up a 'committee of good offices' and by making a very generous proposal to the Jurassian people, namely that the Jurassians themselves should decide whether they wished to retain the status quo, be given autonomy within the canton of Bern or separate fully and form a new canton. The committee was commissioned to draw up a Jura statute and make provision for a separation procedure. There were found to be constitutional difficulties, however, to the giving of autonomy to the Jurassians within the canton of Bern, and, in any case, the Separatists showed no real enthusiasm for the idea.

So in 1970 the Canton of Bern Constitution was amended to allow of a series of votes to settle the matter and this was approved by the Federal Assembly. It was also approved by the people of the canton of Bern.

Successive votes were now taken in the Jura area to determine the wishes of the Jura people, after it had become apparent that the time when an independent state within the canton of Bern would have been accepted as a solution was already past: the points were now set for separation. The people of the Jura were now to decide, firstly, whether they wished a new canton of Jura to be created, and if so, secondly, whether they wished to join that new canton, opt to join a neighbouring canton or preserve the status quo.

At the first vote on 23 June 1974 it was decided to create a new canton, by a narrow majority: the three northern districts, Porrentruy, Franches Montagnes and Delémont voted to form a new canton of Jura, but Laufental and the three southern districts of Courtelary, la Neuveville and Moutier voted against. The next two votes were to determine the boundaries of the new canton. In the first of these the districts of Laufental, Courtelary, la Neuveville and Moutier, in which the vote was held, all voted to stay with Bern, but the majority in the Moutier district was narrow, and so it was decided to allow the communes on the frontier of the new canton to have a third vote to decide which preferred to join the new canton and which desired to stay with Bern. The communes in the north of the Moutier district opted to join the new canton, but the town of Moutier itself and the other communes in the Moutier district, together with two communes in the Delémont district, voted to stay with Bern.

In 1976 a constituent assembly for the new canton of Jura was elected by the voters of the future canton, and the new constitution which they drew up was accepted by the future people in March 1977 and in September 1977 by the Federal Assembly with a reservation.

The revision of the Federal Constitution to provide for the incorporation of the new canton of Jura into the Swiss Confederation was approved by the Federal Assembly in March 1978, and accepted by the whole of the Swiss people and cantons on 24 September 1978.

For a time after this the people of the district of Laufental toyed with the idea of joining a neighbouring canton, but finally, in 1983 they also opted to stay with Bern.

It cannot be assumed that the Jura question was settled once and for all by the creation of a new canton. Many Jurassians regret the fact that the Jura region remains divided, and they were unhappy at the outcome of the plebiscites. If, however, the present settlement does prove to be of only a temporary nature and trouble flares up again in the future, I think that if this conception of federalism continues to be applied and the same magnanimity, broad-mindedness and commonsense are shown in the future as in the past, then a lasting solution will eventually be found.

5

The Militia System

The second especial feature of Swiss life is the militia system. In Switzerland there is no such thing as a professional standing army as the term would be understood in other countries. The Swiss Army is mostly a militia army; it is largely a part-time, semi-professional organization in which the soldiers, for the most part, only receive token payment, but not pay in the true sense of the word. The efficiency and capability of the Swiss Army does not concern us here, but it is important to examine the way it is organized because this so-called militia system is unique to Switzerland, although Israel and Austria have copied certain aspects. It is not only important as regards army organization; it has spilled over and is operative in many other fields of Swiss political and social life.

In the Swiss Army there is a 'hard core' of professional soldiers, a small body of instruction officers, non-commissioned officers for training and a minimum number of personnel for the storage and maintenance of equipment and materials and for administrative purposes: the rest are part-time soldiers.

Military service is compulsory in Switzerland for all Swiss males. If he is not prepared to do his military service a Swiss male must serve a prison sentence unless he is declared medically unfit or is outside Switzerland for legitimate reasons, in which case he will be called upon to pay additional tax. There is no substitute service for military service objectors on grounds of conscience, but out of a total of 650,000 army personnel or thereabouts, there were only 788 conscientious objectors in 1984.

The Swiss Army is an army of defence. As we have seen, after the defeat of the Swiss Army at the Battle of Marignano in 1515, the Swiss withdrew behind their frontiers, and save for a very short exodus during the Hundred Days at the end of the Napoleonic Wars, never again has a Swiss army fought outside

Switzerland under the Swiss flag. After the Battle of Marignano Swiss youth continued to fight as mercenaries in foreign armies in great numbers and Napoleon insisted on Swiss divisions serving in the French Army. It was a Swiss division that helped to extricate the French from Russia in 1812 at the Battle of Beresina, and a Swiss guard fought to the last to defend the French royal family when the Revolutionaries stormed the Tuileries on 10 August 1792. However, for a hundred years now no Swiss person has been allowed to serve in a foreign army save that of the Swiss Papal Guard, if that may be called an army, and in UNO activities.

After an initial training period of seventeen weeks, at the age of twenty, a militia recruit does a three week refresher course for the next eight years, and thereafter periodical refresher courses until the age of fifty (fifty-five for officers). If a recruit wishes to become an officer, he must do an additional initial training in order to attain the rank of 'corporal', and then, if he is adjudged to have the necessary qualities of leadership, he may be accepted to train as an officer; there is no short cut to the officer corps of the Swiss Army. As he rises in rank he will be expected to do a great deal of administrative work voluntarily.

The fact that there is only a small number of professional army personnel, that an ordinary soldier only receives a token payment for his services, and that the officer corps give a proportion of their time voluntarily, means that as far as the army personnel is concerned, the Swiss Army can be run relatively cheaply.

Federalism comes into play, once more, in the equipping of the militia man, for whilst the national authorities provide his weapons, the cantons must provide the soldier's clothing (albeit at national expense), and be responsible for certain annual inspections of both equipment and clothing which the militia man keeps at home. In addition to his refresher course the militia man must attend shooting practices throughout the year.

In peacetime there is no overall commander-in-chief of the Swiss Army. In accordance with the Swiss principle that authority shall be in the hands of the people, the Federal Council has overall authority in respect of the Army and determines what tasks it shall fulfil.

From 1955 to 1982 the cost of the Army to the Federal Exchequer rose from 735 to 3,927 million Swiss francs, which represents roughly twenty per cent of total annual Federal State expenditure.

The Army, however, is only one part of national defence: in this atomic age the population of a country must be defended as well as the national terrain, and consequently, in national defence, civil defence assumes a greater importance. The most important elements of civil defence are air-raid shelters and civil defence rescue squads. In densely populated areas the rescue squads are supported by special army units called air-raid protection troops. Here again federalism is in evidence in the control of these units, because the air-raid protection troops come under the command of the Army Defence Department, but are called into action by a local civilian commander. In medium and small communes, however, civil defence is independent, recruits most of its members from retired people and is under the jurisdiction of the Federal Justice and Police Department.

In addition to providing the defence and security of the country, what other contribution does the militia system make towards helping Switzerland 'tick'?

Firstly, it is an ideal training-ground for Swiss male youth. It is in the recruit-school that many youths first come into contact with collective living, hardship and discipline. It is in the recruit-school that a Swiss youth matures to manhood by his participation in joint endeavour. 'Wait until you get to recruit-school' is apparently a favourite parental admonition in Switzerland.

Secondly, in that the Army is very widely supported by the people, because the militia system binds the Army and the people together, defence policy can be broadly based and count on widespread support from the populace. The militia system is a socially integrating factor, in that youths from all backgrounds and stratas of life meet and live together on equal terms. It gives opportunity for a youth from a less fortunate background, because every boy who comes to recruit-school does, almost literally, 'carry a field marshal's baton in his knapsack'.

Thirdly, by becoming actively involved in the militia system early in life a Swiss youth is more likely to accept it outside the army, and so participate in civic life in a responsible way. In that the Swiss militia army is very much dependent on the officer corps, whose members make tremendous sacrifices in time and in some cases in money too, and in view of the contribution made by trade and industry in supplementing lost earnings during periods of training, the example so set cannot but inculcate a sense of responsibility in all those who participate in this unique type of Swiss organization.

Despite the fact that it is purely a defensive army, I think that a valid criticism can be levelled against the Swiss military system in that no provision is made for the conscientious objector to do some form of civilian service, no matter how onerous that might be. Such a rigid form of compulsion as would appear to appertain here seems in some way to contravene the Swiss conception of the dignity of the person.

It would appear that the Federal Council is fully alive to this criticism, and it may well be that in the none too distant future some form of alternative service may be worked out and accepted by the Swiss people.

6

The Political Institutions

In the composition and functioning of the Swiss political institutions, in addition to the two elements of Swiss statecraft already mentioned, 'federalism' and the 'militia system', a further political principle is evident, namely 'division of power'. Division of power is intended to prevent Federal State authority from falling into too few hands. For this reason it was decreed in the formulation of the Federal Constitution that Federal State authority should be shared by three powers, namely the Legislature (Parliament), the Executive (Government) and the Judiciary (Administration of Justice).

The above three principles of Swiss political statecraft, namely 'federalism', the 'militia system' and a 'division of power' permeate the Swiss political institutions at all levels: national, cantonal and communal.

THE LEGISLATURE

In Switzerland the highest political authority is the Federal Parliament. It consists of two chambers, the National Council representing the people, and the States Council which represents the cantons. The National Council consists of two hundred members, divided between the cantons in proportion to the size of their population. The States Council has forty-six members; each full canton has two seats and each half-canton, one. Both chambers are chosen by the people, but whereas the National Council is elected by the proportional representation voting system, the States Council is elected mainly by the majority voting system. The two chambers are equal in status: all Federal laws and decrees must be authorized by both houses.

The Federal Parliament is composed of members of three large political parties, one medium-sized and various smaller parties. The larger parties are described below, but their description does not necessarily correspond to that of foreign political parties.

| | | | SEATS IN COUNCILS | |
			NATIONAL	STATES
FDP	-	Freisinnig-demokratische Partei der Schweiz (Liberal-Radical)	51	14
CVP	-	Christlichdemokratische Volkspartei der Schweiz (Christian-Democrat)	42	19
SPS	-	Sozialdemokratische Partei der Schweiz (Social-Democrat)	41	5
SVP	-	Schweizerische Volkspartei (Centre party)	25	4
LPS	-	Liberale Partei der Schweiz (Liberal)	9	3
EVP	-	Evangelische Volkspartei der Schweiz (Liberal)	3	
LdU	-	Landesring der Unabhängigen (Independent)	9	1
PDA	-	Partei der Arbeit der Schweiz (Left-wing)	1	
POCH	-	Progressive Organisationen der Schweiz/Grün Alternative	4	
NA	-	Nationale Aktion für Volk und Heimat	3	
		Grüne Parteien (Green parties)	9	
		Andere Parteien (Others)	3	
			200	46

The Swiss Parliament is a militia parliament: there are no full-time members of Parliament in Switzerland. The members of both chambers are part-time politicians who receive little more than their expenses and a nominal reward for their political services. They sacrifice much time to parliamentary work.

The two chambers meeting together form the Federal Assembly, and this is the highest political authority in Switzerland: it is presided over by the President of the National Council. The duties of the Federal Assembly are varied. In time of war, as in the Second World War, the Federal Assembly appoints a commander-in-chief to lead the Army. It appoints the Federal judges and Federal chancellors and sanctions the National Budget. Perhaps its most important function is to elect the Federal Council, which can be variously described as the National Presidium, the Government, the Executive or the Cabinet. It is the task of this body to rule the country.

THE EXECUTIVE – THE FEDERAL COUNCIL

The Federal Council is composed of seven members from four different political parties. The composition of the Federal Council is known as the 'magic formula' and has been in operation since 1959: it consists of two members of each of the following parties, Freisinnig-demokratische Partei der Schweiz (Liberal-Radical), Christlichdemokratische Volkspartei der Schweiz (Christian-Democrat) and Sozialdemokratische Partei der Schweiz (Social-Democrat) and one member from the Schweizerische Volkspartei (Centre party mostly representing farmers and small business). The fact that the Swiss Government is so broadly-based makes for stability, which is highly-prized by the Swiss. It means that the parties represented in the Federal Council are supported by more than three-quarters of the members of Parliament. It has been deemed the most stable government in the world. In determining the composition of the Federal Council the political parties are not the only criterion: an unwritten law stipulates that two of them should stem from the Italian, French or Romanisch-speaking areas of the country, and also that the large cantons of Zurich, Bern and Vaud should normally be represented.

The stability of the Government also ensues from the fact that a Federal councillor is not easily deprived of office by Parliament: it would have to be something serious to remove him. This is because in the Swiss Parliament there is no such thing as a vote of 'no confidence' in respect of Federal councillors, because the Federal Council is run on the collegial system. Each minister is the head of one of seven departments: Foreign Affairs, Home Affairs, Justice and Police, Military, Finance, Economic Affairs, Transport and Energy. In the Federal Council all decisions are taken jointly and responsibility is shared.

The main task of the Federal Council is to govern the country: it is therefore head of the Administration, and as such has at its disposal a large body of civil servants, some 34,000. Because it has access to such a wealth of reference and expertise, it has an advantage over the two houses of Parliament.

In Switzerland there is no official head of state. The nearest approach is the President of the Federal Council, but he is only allowed to be President for one year and has no real authority. Throughout his year of office he remains head of a department, and at the end of his term of office reverts back to being one of the seven, and a fellow cabinet minister takes his place as President.

In the House of Parliament we find the Federal Chancellery, which is the equivalent of the Cabinet Office. The Federal Chancellor (or Secretary General) and his two vice-chancellors are responsible for the most important head-quarters work of the Federal Council and also for public relations. The Federal Chancellor attends Federal Council meetings in an advisory capacity.

Many of the enactments passed by Parliament originate in Parliament itself, and are usually initiated by a member of the National Council or by one of the States Council. The ball is usually set in motion by one of these instigating a request by Parliament to the Federal Council to work out a draft-measure to be re-submitted to Parliament for debate. If the request is in the form of a 'motion' and has the approval of both chambers, then the Federal Council is compelled to work out a draft-measure; if it is in the form of a 'postulate', then the Federal Council is merely required to consider whether it should do so or not. The Federal Council having decided to do so, then experts are called in to draft an outline measure. This is then sent to the cantons and also exposed to a general hearing (Vernehmlassung), where the cantons, political parties and interest groups are allowed to express an opinion on it and recommend improvements. Having taken note of these and various other reports, the Federal Council can then amend the draft-measure accordingly and present it to the Houses of Parliament. It is then decided which chamber shall debate it first, and that chamber then appoints an inter-party committee to discuss the measure in detail. This is then submitted to the parliamentary parties and presented for debate in the first chamber. After this it is sent to the second chamber and here the same procedure is repeated. Differences between the two houses are ironed out in an harmonization procedure. If it is then accepted by both houses it is returned to the Federal Council, which either brings it into force legally or submits it to the required referendum.

7

The Judiciary

The Judiciary in Switzerland is an independent authority. At national level it is represented by the Federal Supreme Court, which in 1874, in order to emphasize the division of political power and the independence of the Judiciary, was housed in Lausanne rather than in Bern.

It is a college of around thirty judges and certain substitute judges elected to serve for six years. Its independence of the Government is undisputed: influence can only be exerted on it in the appointment of the judges by the Federal Assembly. Otherwise the judges are independent, for like federal councillors it is not easy to get rid of them, and also like the latter they are not allowed to follow any other occupation. The Federal Constitution insists that all three official languages be represented in the Federal Supreme Court.

The duty of the Federal Supreme Court is to 'administer justice'. It is the highest judicial authority in the land, and as such the only or final court of appeal in civil, constitutional and administrative legal disputes. With a jury it adjudicates in cases of high treason, infringements of international law and in political crimes and offences. It adjudicates in disputes between the cantons, and acts as a court of appeal for any citizen who feels that he has been wronged constitutionally by a cantonal or communal authority.

The method of organization of the Federal Supreme Court is like that of the Federal Council. It is divided up into specialist chambers and the cases are apportioned accordingly.

The most important of Swiss laws, the civil and penal code, are federal laws, but the courts which administer these are, for the most part, cantonal, and they vary in procedure from canton to canton.

The communes play no important role in the administration of the law. The first real courts are the district courts, and above these are the cantonal courts: these usually comprise a high court, an assize court, a court of appeal, a commercial court and an administrative court. At this level, if the case is serious, the Federal State authorities as guardians of the public interest may step in, and if necessary prosecute in a district or cantonal court. The execution of the sentence is the responsibility of the cantons.

The Federal Insurance Court should also be mentioned: it is an independent social security court within the Federal Supreme Court. It deals with disputes in respect of social insurance and military insurance, usually as a court of appeal. Lastly there are military courts in Switzerland which adjudicate on violations of the military penal code.

8

Neutrality

Perhaps the greatest blessing which has been conferred on Switzerland during the past century is peace, both external and internal. The fact that external peace has been preserved is due to Switzerland's excellent defences, a certain amount of good fortune, but above all to her policy of permanent neutrality. For the Swiss independence and neutrality have become inseparable.

As we have seen, after the defeat of the Swiss at the Battle of Marignano, in 1515, which was so decisive, the Swiss people began to learn the lesson that aggression is a hazardous business: they withdrew within their own frontiers and slowly adopted a policy of neutrality. This policy of abstention from foreign involvement was of value to Switzerland during the religious wars which followed in Europe, because, as we have seen, half of her population adopted the new faith, Protestantism, and the other half remained true to the old faith, Catholicism. Again, as ethnically the Swiss people largely represent three different national backgrounds, based on three nations which border on her frontiers, if Switzerland's foreign policy had not been one of neutrality the country would have been torn apart later in each of the major European wars.

Switzerland's permanent neutrality was first acknowledged at the Congress of Vienna in 1815, but in order to obtain acceptance for it from the European powers Switzerland had to negotiate, and in these negotiations cede certain of her territory, so that this is a negotiated agreement which contains a guarantee from the European powers that should be respected. The Hague Convention of 1907 stipulated that this permanent neutrality of Switzerland should be a defended neutrality. Switzerland's permanent neutrality was again confirmed in Article 435 of the Treaty of Versailles in 1919.

Permanent neutrality was written into the Swiss Federal Constitution of 1848 but it does not give an interpretation of 'neutrality'. It does say, however, that it is the duty of the Federal Government to guarantee it. In 1848 the cantons only relinquished their right to negotiate with foreign powers on condition that the Federal State adopted a policy of permanent neutrality. Such a policy is, therefore, essential to the preservation of the Swiss Confederation. It means that Switzerland must refrain from participation in any treaties, offensive or defensive, which carry with them a risk of war, however remote. This does not debar her, however, from joining in international humanitarian work or from helping developing countries.

The benefits which a policy of permanent neutrality brings to Switzerland are firstly that it ensures non-intervention for Switzerland in foreign affairs which carry any threat of war. Secondly it is a requirement for internal peace between the cantons. Thirdly, it is an instrument in safeguarding Switzerland's economic existence, because being short of raw materials Switzerland is economically dependent on the outside world: by being permanently neutral Switzerland can more readily obtain the food and raw materials she depends on.

The major benefit for the outside world of Switzerland's permanent neutrality is that it is of service to international peace-keeping. It means that Switzerland can represent and protect the interests of nations in dispute, and can also keep a permanent dialogue and negotiations going between warring factions. At the beginning of 1982 Switzerland had sixteen such mandates.

That this neutrality has remained permanent is largely due to the self-interest of the European powers. In the seventeenth and eighteenth centuries it was in France's interest to have a buffer zone between herself and the Habsburg empire. During these two centuries it was also essential for the princely houses of Europe to have a guaranteed source of supply of mercenaries to replenish their armies when they were depleted in battle: if Switzerland had been at war herself this would have been out of the question. In the two World Wars it would appear to have been in the interest of both sides to have Switzerland neutral.

The universality principle, which is closely connected to the neutrality principle, also guides Switzerland's foreign policy. It requires that Switzerland should have diplomatic contacts with as many countries as possible, irrespective of the colour or complexion of their government.

A further principle upon which Switzerland's foreign policy is based has already been touched upon, namely availability, that is of making her good offices available to any parties in dispute. Switzerland represents several governments, and many international organizations are domiciled in Switzerland: Swiss citizens are leading figures in some of these organizations. Switzerland also acts as host to many international conferences.

Switzerland is not a member of UNO. She is, however, a member of the Council of Europe. She also concluded a treaty of association with the Common Market, but only after strictly safeguarding her right of autonomy. Switzerland is also a member of the European Free Trade Association, because this is purely a commercial organization.

9

The Red Cross

Permanent neutrality in Switzerland, therefore, is prompted by a domestic necessity and an international requirement. It does not mean the adoption of an attitude of indifference to what goes on abroad, nor is this military and political non-intervention motivated purely by self-interest. This is shown by the founding of the Red Cross Movement by Henri Dunant, a Geneva merchant, at the Battle of Solferino in 1859. On witnessing the slaughter in that battle he was prompted to do something about it, and started tending the wounded as best he could. Some neighbouring women were amazed to see him assisting both sides, irrespective of nationality, and with their continual comment 'tutti fratelli' (all are brothers) they expressed the idea upon which the Red Cross Movement was to be based. Five years later Dunant persuaded sixteen states to sign the first Geneva Convention to alleviate suffering in war, and thereby he founded the Red Cross Movement.

In view of Switzerland's neutrality and her humanitarian work, it is not surprising that Geneva has become one of the main centres of international endeavour.

10

Humanitarian Work

Throughout the ages Switzerland has served as a place of asylum for religious and political refugees: many renowned people have sought refuge within her borders. The greatest number of refugees came as a result of war: the Franco-Prussian and the two World Wars. Although during the Second World War many refugees had to be refused entry because of a shortage of food, after the War, between 1944 and 1948, Switzerland contributed Sfr 200 million to the rehabilitation of Europe. Private institutions and individuals participate extensively in Swiss refugee work: the childrens' Pestalozzi village in Trogen offers a good example of Swiss effort in this field.

Switzerland is also involved in Overseas Development Aid, both directly and indirectly through United Nations agencies. Aid is offered directly in the form of financial assistance, technical co-operation and advice, and in trade measures such as preferential customs treatment for certain goods from Third World countries.

Switzerland has also developed her own programme for overseas humanitarian assistance in the event of natural catastrophe.

11

Interest Groups and Trade Unions —

Social Legislation

Another secret of Switzerland's prosperity is that social harmony has prevailed in Switzerland for many years. The fact that there has been industrial peace for so long is largely attributable to the good sense, moderation and willingness to compromise on the part of the Swiss employers' associations and trade unions, and also to the excellent machinery which they have devised for mediation when disputes do arise.

The tradition of negotiation and mediation goes back to the foundation of the Swiss Confederation in the Rütli meadow in 1291. The Federal Letter signed here provides for the settling of disputes: it clearly states, 'If, however, discord should arise between Swiss confederates, then the most prudent of the Swiss confederates are to mediate and arbitrate in the dispute, and if one of the parties should reject the verdict of these arbitrators, then the rest of the confederates must ensure that the verdict is complied with by the rebellious party'.

Several trade unions were founded by religious organizations, and this too has meant that their attitudes have been less radical than those in some other countries. The Swiss trade unions are less ideological and more practical: their motivation is more economic than political. The largest group of trade unions is the Swiss Trade Union Alliance: it has close relations with the Social-Democratic party, but there are smaller unions which have ties with some of the other political parties.

The employers have their associations that work closely with various political parties. They have representatives in those parties at both national and cantonal level. Parliament and the 'general hearing' are where the employers and trade union organizations exert their influence, rather than through political parties. Yet all the important employers' associations and trade unions enjoy very close relations with political parties, and before general elections they negotiate with them to have their members nominated as candidates.

The employers' associations and trade unions are explicitly mentioned in the Federal Constitution: the political authorities are required to plan and execute their economic policy in agreement with the social partners. The Federal State plays no part in private wage negotiations, but after an agreement has been reached, in many instances the Federal Government can declare an agreement as universally binding.

The trade unions and employers' associations in Switzerland are manifestly sensible: they obviously realize that the 'cake' has to be baked before it can be shared out and that to refuse to bake it through strike-action is folly and in the end benefits no one. Only once have trade unions joined forces with the Social-Democratic party to take direct action and that was in the General Strike of 1918, which was led by the 'Olten Committee'. The strike was declared illegal by the Federal Council and was over in three days, but the demands which were made by the 'Olten Committee' have since all been met and are now all incorporated in Swiss law.

The commonsense attitude of the trade unions and the employers' associations is best exemplified by the 1937 Peace Agreement made on 19 July 1937 between the employers' associations and the trade unions in the metal and watch-making industry. Both were loath to have the Government intervene in their dispute, and so they came to an agreement whereby strikes and lock-outs would henceforth be banned: future disputes were to be settled by negotiation, and if this were found to be impossible then the matter should be referred to an impartial conciliation court and the findings of this court should be binding on both parties. Each side deposited Sfr 250,000 in an account at the Swiss National Bank as security, and it was agreed that if either side violated the agreement then its deposit money should be forfeit. This agreement has continued to be honoured by both parties and it has set an example for other industries. The result is that there has been no major strike in Switzerland since that day.

There is criticism in Switzerland of the influence which interest-groups and trade unions exercise on political life. Some go so far as to say that they rule the country. Against this it should be pointed out that surely it is sensible for national legislators to allow of a ventilation of criticism and opposition to any proposed measure at an early stage in the legislation procedure. Secondly, that the interest-groups and trade unions do represent a very wide spectrum of Swiss life and so should be taken account of, and thirdly, that no matter what influence is brought to bear on the legislators to modify legislative proposals, the people themselves are the final arbitrators. As we shall see in an ensuing chapter, they have the power to reject any piece of legislation which is passed by Parliament.

But the industrial harmony which prevails in Switzerland is also due to the social policies which have been pursued by the Government. At the time of the founding of the Federal State, in 1848, the Liberal-Radicals were at the helm in Switzerland and liberal policies held sway. One of the tenets of liberal philosophy maintained that economic forces should have free play: that competition would solve all the country's economic problems. Poverty was viewed as an indictment of the individual, and was regarded as being of no concern of the State. As industrialization progressed, however, it was realized that working conditions in the factories could not just be left as they were, and also that provision must be made for the poor in times of economic recession. So the Federal State was compelled to intervene with suitable social policies which at first only involved factory workers, but which during the next hundred years were extended to include all the working population.

The law of obligation, which was introduced in 1883, has proved to be a very powerful instrument in determining and promoting contractual undertakings between employer and employee in Switzerland.

Factory laws were introduced in 1877 and 1914 which improved working conditions in the factories tremendously, and additions were made over the years until in 1966 a comprehensive factory law was introduced which covers maximum working hours, overtime, unsocial working hours, paid holidays etc. In addition, in many concerns there are extended private agreements.

In 1919, Accident Insurance (UV) was introduced. Insurance against accidents is compulsory for all employees in Switzerland. Since 1919 the Swiss Accident Insurance Institute

(SUVA) in Lucerne, a private organization, has run this department of social security. The first paid holidays were brought in for apprentices and female workers in Bern in 1905 and 1908.

The privation suffered by soldiers' families in the First World War, which was a major cause of the General Strike in 1918, prompted the Federal Government in 1939, when the outbreak of the Second World War was imminent, to introduce a compensation insurance fund for a soldier's loss of earnings as a result of being called up: it is called the Earnings Indemnity Regulation (EO). This went a long way towards helping to alleviate similar hardship to soldiers' families in the Second World War and to obviate social unrest. After the Second World War it was extended to cover all militia men and Civil Defence conscripts on being called up.

In 1947, the Old Age and Bereavement (Widows and Orphans) Insurance (AHV) was introduced, to provide retirement pensions and pensions for widows and orphans and this has proved to be a most popular piece of Swiss social legislation. Since 1947 it has been extended until in 1979 more was paid out in AHV payments than the whole of the Swiss national income in 1939.

Two other forms of compulsory insurance for Swiss employees are the Disablement Insurance (IV), which covers the risk of being invalided and is used to provide rehabilitation facilities for the disabled: if rehabilitation proves to be impossible, then an invalid pension is paid. The second is Unemployment Insurance (AV), which helps to compensate for loss of earnings in the event of partial or full unemployment.

The provision for social welfare in Switzerland is made in a variety of ways. Old age is catered for by what is known as the 'three pillar' system. The first pillar is the Old Age and Bereavement (Widows and Orphans) Insurance (AHV), the second the Occupational Provision for Old Age, Disablement and Bereavement (Widows and Orphans), known as (BV), and the third is the provision made for old age by the individual himself.

The first pillar is financed by a percentage deduction from wages or salaries (to which is added a similar amount by the employer), by contributions by the Federal State and cantons and from interest on AHV investments. Disablement Insurance is linked to AHV and is financed in the same way. The second pillar is financed solely by a percentage deduction from wages and salaries plus a similar amount from the employer. The third pillar is financed by the individual himself. Other forms of social insurance, namely Unemployment Insurance, Earnings Indemnity, Accident Insurance and Health Insurance, where it is compulsory, are also financed by a percentage deduction from wages and salaries, to which is added a similar amount by the employer: in exceptional circumstances the Federal State and the cantons may also contribute towards Unemployment Insurance. All contributions made by tax-payers to social insurance in Switzerland qualify for tax relief. All this social insurance in Switzerland is administered through numerous Federal, cantonal and private insurance funds, known as Ausgleichs or Krankenkassen, as well as by private insurance companies.

12

Health Insurance

In keeping with the Swiss tradition of personal freedom, insurance against sickness has never been made universally compulsory in Switzerland. The people have rejected compulsion at various referenda, but most cantons are free to introduce compulsory health insurance for certain groups of the population. As a result of this and of the extensive amount of private health insurance taken out by the Swiss, the percentage of those insured against sickness is very high, namely around ninety-eight per cent of the populace. This private health insurance is largely organized by numerous private sick-benefit funds. For those who cannot insure there is a social safety net which ensures that no Swiss person need be homeless, go hungry or lack medical care. The Swiss medical services per head of the population compare favourably with those of other countries: in 1985 there were 913 hospitals nationwide and 16,473 doctors in practice.

As a result of this extensive social legislation, unrest in Switzerland would appear to have been reduced to a minimum, and thanks to prosperity poverty has been largely abolished.

The provision of social security in Switzerland has been emphasized because sometimes foreigners seem to have the impression that in Switzerland little is done by the authorities to counter the hazards of life. This is not true: the difference between Switzerland and those countries with compulsory state health insurance schemes is that the Swiss prefer, if possible, to stand on their own two legs rather than have the Federal State intervene.

13

The Tax System

At the founding of the Swiss Federal State in 1848, the Federal State was allowed the revenue from customs dues and monopolies to meet its expenses. It was envisaged that the cantons would have to make a proportionate contribution to Federal finances. In practice, however, it soon became apparent that the income accruing from customs dues and monopolies would far exceed what had been estimated: that no monies would be required from the cantons, but rather that the Federal State would have a surplus of revenue, that it would be able to meet its own needs and that there would be a certain amount left to distribute between the cantons.

The Federal Council is compelled to submit its proposals on expenditure for the ensuing year to Parliament, and Parliament must debate these proposals in the December session.

The fact that the Federal Government is in a position to subsidize the cantons does give it a certain influence over them that it would not otherwise have.

It is not intended here to give a detailed account of taxation in Switzerland: suffice it to say that, in accordance with the federal principle, taxes are levied by the Federal State, the cantons and the communes, and yet despite this Switzerland is regarded as being a fairly low-taxed country. In Switzerland, however, there are concealed impositions which should be taken into account if a true tax comparison is to be made with other countries: the reference here is to the higher than normal prices which the people have to pay on certain farm products in order to help to cover subsidies to agriculture.

14

Education

As in other European countries, education in Switzerland is compulsory and universal. The Federal Constitution states 'that the cantons shall provide adequate primary school instruction', that it shall be under Federal State supervision, compulsory, free and accessible to children of all confessions without prejudice to freedom of belief or conscience.

The fact that almost ninety-five per cent of all Swiss children attend these schools ensures a very large degree of equality of opportunity for the Swiss child. In that the responsibility for education is largely the commitment of the cantons means that in the ordering of school life there are variations from canton to canton.

A Swiss child commences his or her education in the kindergarten, but his or her compulsory education starts at the age of six or seven when these children enter primary school. After four to six years in primary school, which varies according to the canton, the child is offered a wide choice of curriculum on entering an intermediate school, and this may finally lead to an apprenticeship in trade or industry plus vocational education, to a college of technology or to a university. There are twenty-seven advanced colleges of technology in Switzerland and ten universities: eight of the latter are run by the cantons and two by the Federal State. There is also a university of pedagogics in St Gallen and a theological faculty in Lucerne. The cantons are responsible for the appointment and training of teachers. In Switzerland the aim is, quite simply, to make the best possible education available to every child by means of a fair scholarship and student grant system.

15

Vocational Training and Apprenticeship

Before a youth leaves school in Switzerland at the end of his or her fifteenth year, he or she will probably already have had talks in school from a professional careers officer and also, perhaps, personal guidance from him too, as to what career he or she should embark on. The Swiss appear to be anxious that their children should not end up as 'square pegs in round holes', and in order to obviate this where possible, the Swiss Federal authorities, in co-operation with the cantons and professional and trade associations, have set up a careers advisory service which is at the disposal of all school-leavers and older people.

If the youth chooses a career in trade, industry, commerce, the service industries or domestic science, it is likely that he or she will have been advised to take an apprenticeship in order to equip themselves for their future career. It is because of the heavy emphasis on apprenticeship in Switzerland that so many people do become apprenticed, and it is because so many people serve an apprenticeship that the percentage of qualified workers in Switzerland is higher than in most countries.

Basic vocational training in Switzerland provides the necessary competence and knowledge for the pursuit of a vocation. It extends general education, furthers the development of personality and promotes a sense of responsibility. It also provides the basis for general and specialized further education.

Basic vocational training is usually effected by means of an apprenticeship and is given at a private or public place of work by the employer himself, if he is a qualified master of his trade, or by some other qualified person working in that establishment. This is coupled with part-time education at a vocational training-school where the necessary theoretical knowledge is given. It may also be effected by means of an apprenticeship in a training-workshop or school of design which also give vocational teaching alongside practical training, or at a public or private charitable intermediate college of commerce whose final examination is recognized by the Federal authorities.

A Swiss youth may commence vocational training after he or she has completed their fifteenth year, and the initial course lasts at least two years and usually three or four. Only qualified teachers may instruct in vocational training courses, and the organization and supervision of these courses is effected by the cantonal authorities.

Contracts of apprenticeship between the employer and the apprentice are drawn up before the course starts, and these must be sanctioned by the cantonal authority. In these contracts of apprenticeship, or indentures, the conditions of the apprenticeship are laid down in detail: these include rates of pay, conditions of service, the obligations of both parties to the agreement and those of the cantonal authorities.

At the end of the course the apprentice must take an examination, and if he passes he will receive a certificate of proficiency which will certify that he is now a skilled worker in that occupation.

Swiss youth who are predominantly practical are also given the opportunity of taking a semi-skilled apprenticeship for at least one year in order to acquire skills in simple manufacturing and industrial processes. At the end of the course the semi-skilled apprentice will receive an official certificate of proficiency.

16

Intermediate Schools of Commerce

There are also intermediate schools of commerce which offer three or four year courses which consist of further general education together with professional instruction, in order to equip students for a position in a commercial firm, the service industries or the Administration. Whoever completes this course and passes the final examination will receive a diploma. For those apprentices and semi-skilled apprentices who have completed their basic training, there exists the opportunity of continuing their vocational education at an intermediate vocational training school. After a further two years' work and study a student may take further examinations.

17

The Professional and Advanced Specialist Examinations

Professional and trade organizations may request that further examinations be held, namely Professional Examinations (Berufsprüfungen) and Advanced Specialist Examinations (Fachprüfungen). The Professional Examination is intended to determine whether the candidate has the necessary vocational skills and knowledge to occupy a managerial position or fulfil a professional task which demands more expertise than would be expected from a person with only a basic vocational training. The Advanced Specialist Examination is intended to indicate whether a person is capable of managing a business on his own or of fulfilling more demanding tasks in his vocation. The examinations are supervised by the Federal authorities. Whoever passes the Professional Examination will receive a professional certificate (Fachausweis), and those who are successful in the Advanced Specialist Examination receive a diploma: all their names are published and entered in an official register which is open for inspection.

—————— **18** ——————

Advanced Vocational Education

Advanced vocational education is given mostly in the following educational establishments:

a) Schools of Engineering which equip students for the undertaking of industrial tasks and for management at intermediate level. At the end of the course, if they pass the final examination, they will receive the title of 'Technical Engineer TS' (Techniker TS).

b) Advanced Colleges of Technology (Schools of Engineering) where the theory and practice of engineering, mathematics, natural science, the science of engineering, building technology, architecture and general studies are taught. The students by following these studies equip and enable themselves to apply the findings of science and research to industrial production and development, or to apply them independently in other specialist fields. Whoever completes this course and passes the final examination of an Advanced College of Technology will receive the designation 'Engineer HTL' (Ingenieur HTL).

c)Advanced Schools of Economics and Management which teach the basics of economic science and give a further general education. This is intended to give the student the necessary skill and knowledge to deal with the demanding economic problems of business management in trade and industry and in the Administration. Whoever completes this course and passes the final examination will be entitled to call himself 'Business Economist HWV' (Betriebsökonom HWV).

There are also other Advanced Schools of Technology which the Federal State subsidizes: it also promotes vocational training research.

In Switzerland an average youth would appear to accept the fact that vocational education and training after leaving school are both desirable and necessary. This attitude is also encouraged by the fact that in Swiss vocational life remuneration is geared to qualification: the more qualified a person is, the higher will be his or her salary.

The result of this carefully planned and extensive vocational training in Switzerland is that very many Swiss employees have a qualification: over-seers, almost without exception, have a basic training qualification and many have a further vocational training diploma also. The high standard of vocational education in Switzerland gives the country a tremendous economic advantage. In that it also includes further general education, it also helps to equip Swiss citizens with the necessary means to take the social and political decisions which a semi-direct democracy requires of them.

Such extensive further education of the Swiss work-force would not have been possible had Switzerland not had access to a plentiful supply of foreign workers who were willing to perform less qualified tasks. Fortunately since 1950 this has presented no problem, because since that date there has been a continual flow of foreigners to Switzerland seeking jobs. In 1986 there were altogether 788,000 foreigners working in Switzerland: these consisted of around 432,000 who were permanently resident here, 126,000 with a year's work-permit, 110,000 seasonal workers and 120,000 who cross the frontier daily to work in Switzerland.

Vocational education and apprenticeship have been stressed here, probably at the expense of other forms of education, because they are so widespread and because it is widely thought in Switzerland that the educating of the Swiss work-force is the key to Switzerland's economic success. Switzerland has a very long tradition of vocational training which has had to be adapted to fresh knowledge and new ideas.

19

Swiss Economic Philosophy —

The Public and Private Sectors

The Swiss would appear to be, for the most part, firm believers in a market economy, that is in capitalism. This, no doubt, stems from their love of freedom and independence and from a practical way of looking at things. It would seem that for the great majority of the Swiss, capitalism and democracy go hand in hand. They believe, too, in competition which is the concomitant of a free market economy, because where competition is abolished the incentive for innovation and perfection is destroyed. Many believe that competition in trade and industry gives added choice to the consumer by increasing the variety of products offered, and that it also helps to satisfy new needs. It is an aid in eliminating the manufacture of articles for which there is no further demand, and acts as an incentive to technical perfection and new discoveries. It is freely acknowledged in Switzerland that competitive effort has contributed greatly to the enriching of the Swiss people: where there is no competition or striving for profit, as in socialist countries with centralized economies, the incentive to perfection is lacking, and shortages can soon arise which in turn may lead to rationing.

The majority of Swiss people would appear to reject the socialist idea that the enriching of one person leads inevitably to the impoverishment of another. In that an ostentatious display of wealth or a striving after social exclusiveness would appear to be unacceptable to the average Swiss person, if he or she does make money their first inclination seems to be to put it in the bank. This money is then available to their fellows as credit, so that they too may enrich themselves in turn, and as credit is available from the Swiss banks at one of the lowest rates in Europe, this creates widespread opportunity. The most fitting analogy is that of a roped climbing-team – the strongest climbs first and prepares the way for the less competent to follow.

But competition is easily abused, as the Swiss are aware, and if fair play is to be maintained it is essential that the Federal State should keep a close watch on proceedings.

In Switzerland a 'nationalization philosophy' has never taken root: there have always had to be irrefutable grounds for the taking of a competency out of private hands and conferring it on the Federal State. In certain circumstances, throughout the years, such actions have been adequately justified, as a result of which the Federal State has taken over additional functions, and therefore over the years a workable system of co-existence has had to be worked out between the public and private sectors of the Swiss economy, until today they are almost inextricably enmeshed together. Nevertheless, much that belongs to the public sector in other countries lies within the province of private industry in Switzerland.

In Switzerland an attempt is made to have as many people as possible gainfully employed: usually the figure varies between forty-five per cent and fifty per cent of the total population. On the 1st January 1986 out of a total population of 6,484,800, there were slightly fewer than 3,200,000 gainfully employed, full-time.

But Switzerland seems to go further than most countries in laying emphasis on having as many people as possible directly involved in creating the wherewithal to live, that is in the immediate making and baking of the national 'cake'. Every effort is made to restrict the number of people employed in public administration to a minimum, and by international standards that number is modest.

Switzerland is committed to a market economy, to capitalism: it is written into the Federal Constitution of 1874. This had to be altered to allow the Federal State to intervene in economic affairs as and when this was deemed to be in the public interest, but this intervention must be restricted to a minimum. The Swiss are still firmly committed to a liberal market economy. The Federal State and trade and industry work together as partners in the creation of Switzerland's prosperity.

20

Trade and Industry

During the past 100 years Swiss trade and industry has developed tremendously. As has already been mentioned, Switzerland has few natural resources and previously she had great difficulty in feeding her population. For centuries she gleaned a bare existence from agriculture, a certain amount from industry, from the trade routes which crossed her territory and by hiring her sons as mercenaries to foreign armies.

The tide turned and her fortunes changed when the emphasis in the Swiss national economy moved from agriculture to manufacturing industry, and also when this was later supplemented by a surge in tourism. A hundred years ago almost half the Swiss population was engaged in agriculture: today it is less than six per cent. Since the Second World War alone the number of those employed in trade and industry has increased by fifty per cent. The prosperity which has ensued from this industrial transformation is shown by the fact that whereas in 1925 an average Swiss worker had to work six hours to earn one kg of butter, by 1980 he need only work one hour.

This huge transformation from agriculture to manufacturing industry, however, was only made possible by the discovery of a new source of energy, namely electricity. Hitherto, the only sources of energy which Switzerland had possessed other than water had been a limited amount of coal and a plentiful supply of timber. Her mills and factories had to be housed on the banks of rivers and streams. The discovery of the Girard turbine in Vevey in 1863, however, brought with it the possibility of harnessing Switzerland's enormous water potential: by building dams the water from the melting winter snows could be collected and fed through sluices, as required, to produce electricity, and after a German, Werner von Siemens, had produced his first electrical-exciter in 1866, which was the forerunner of the modern electric-generator, it became possible for electricity to be fed throughout the country.

An English engineer named Brown and a German engineer named Boveri, who was perhaps the first person to appreciate the vastness of Switzerland's water potential, joined forces to found their own electrical engineering firm in Baden in 1891. Today, Brown Boveri and Co AG is the most important electrical engineering firm in Switzerland. With the discovery of the electric motor and direct current the way lay open for the electrification of Switzerland, and the discovery of this cheap source of universal energy gave a tremendous economic advantage to Swiss industry.

After the Second World War Switzerland was fortunate in having the necessary requirements for a dramatic economic leap forward: her factories had emerged from the War unscathed and she had the required labour-force and capital at her disposal. She poured money into industrial research, new technology and the education of her work-force. The result was that in twenty years, from 1964 to 1984, her Gross National Product (GNP) increased by over fifty per cent.

21

The Textile and Clothing Industry

The Swiss textile industry is the oldest of the Swiss industries: it stretches back to the Middle Ages. At that time silk was processed in Zurich and cloth was manufactured in Fribourg: the linen industry was domiciled in St Gallen and the cotton industry developed here later, too.

Spinning and weaving were originally mostly carried out in the homes of the people, as were clock and watch-making. This domestic part-time work was of great benefit to the people in times of poor harvests because it meant that the Swiss peasants were not wholly dependent on agriculture for their livelihood.

It remained largely a home industry until two Englishmen, John Heywood and James Longworth, were persuaded to come to St Gallen and bring with them English spinning and weaving expertise. The first Swiss mechanized spinning mill was established by them in St Gallen Monastery in 1801 and with it a repair-shop, because with Napoleon's economic blockade of England, spare parts for the Swiss 'spinning-jenny' were hard to obtain from England. In 1805 followed the founding of the Escher Wyss firm in Zurich, together with a repair-shop and machine-construction factory. It was in this way that a mechanized textile industry was gradually established. The industry had to face stiff opposition from England, but nevertheless it grew, and by the outbreak of the First World War was exporting Sfr 215,000,000 worth of embroidery work annually: at that time this represented sixteen per cent of all Swiss exports.

Swiss fabrics are now renowned throughout the world. St Gallen embroidery, Zurich silk and such fabrics as muslin, gaberdines, organdie and voile are the products which have brought fame to the Swiss textile industry. Although, from time to time, the Swiss textile industry has had to trim its sails to the biting winds of foreign competition and adapt quickly, thanks to the investing of huge sums in modern machinery as it became available, it has steadily progressed.

At the end of 1979 the Swiss textile and clothing industry was employing 65,000 people in more than a thousand firms. These firms are mostly situated in eastern Switzerland. In 1979 exports in the textile and clothing industry equalled those of the clock and watch-making industry, but whereas the latter exported ninety per cent of its production in that year, the textile and clothing industry exported only forty per cent.

Today the textile and clothing industry is Switzerland's third largest industry.

22

The Machine and Metal Industry

The machine and metal industry is by far the largest industry in Switzerland: it employs around forty-eight per cent of all those in work in industry, and is responsible for about forty-five per cent of all Swiss exports. It comprises very small firms and huge multinational companies such as Brown Boveri, von Roll, Sulzer Bros etc. Its products range from small precision instruments to large turbines for ocean-going liners: from lifts in hotels to cable cars and huge electric generators.

There had already been foundries in Switzerland for many years, but machine-building only began at the beginning of the nineteenth century. Its origins were two fold. Firstly, during the Napoleonic Wars when an economic blockade was imposed on England, it was difficult for the Swiss textile industry to get spare parts for its looms, or, when necessary, to replace them, and consequently repair-shops and machine-foundries had to be established locally. Secondly, it was made possible by Johann Conrad Fischer's developing of a foundry in Mühlental, near Schaffhausen, in 1802, by using local iron-ore. He was the founder of the Fischer Group of companies which in 1981 employed almost 17,000 people. A little later a certain Baron von Roll established a foundry in Solothurn with French capital. When, after the defeat of Napoleon in 1815, French capital dried up, he had to reorganize his business in 1823 by using Swiss capital. Around 1830 the Sulzer brothers entered the foundry business in Winterthur. Among their other activities they began to build steamships, but when in 1879 a laboratory assistant named Diesel joined the firm he brought with him his ideas for the development of the diesel motor, and this gradually replaced steam. Today Sulzer Bros equip a large part of the world's sea-going ships with their diesel-engines.

In 1860 a certain Adolf Bühler established a foundry in Uzwil and in 1872 succeeded in making the first casted rolling-drum for grinding corn. Later the firm went on to the building of loading and unloading dock equipment and silo buildings: they also diversified into the building of machines for the food industry. Bühlers are now the largest firm in the world for the construction of grinding-mills, and Sulzer Bros are the world premier firm for the building of diesel marine engines. That a Swiss firm so far from the sea should become so prominent in marine engineering is a tribute to the enterprise and resource of the Swiss people.

Swiss technical inventions in the machine industry include the discovery of the turbo-generator (1898), the electrical rack-and-pinnion railway (1890), the pump-turbine (1930) and the gas-turbine power-station in 1978.

23

The Chemical and Pharmaceutical Industry

Another giant Swiss industry is the chemical and pharmaceutical industry: it is spread over the whole of Switzerland.

Already, in the Middle Ages, alchemists were active in Switzerland, but it was Paracelsus at Einsiedeln, in the sixteenth century, who brought chemistry more into prominence with his experiments as a part of medicine. It was, however, only after the discovery of the molecular construction of dyestuffs, in the middle of the last century, that the chemical industry really began to expand, and the stimulus for the expansion of the industry came from the manufacture of textiles.

As Switzerland herself played almost no part in the discovery of synthetic dyestuffs, she had to rely on foreign expertise. This came in part from a Frenchman named Clavel who settled in Basel in 1859. It was he who founded the business which was later to become Ciba (Chemical Industry of Basel) and which eventually merged with Geigy in 1970. Geigy had been in business in Basel since 1758, but it was only in 1859 that they had gone over to the manufacture of synthetic dyestuffs.

Sandoz and Kern also founded their business in Basel about this time (1886) for the manufacture of dyestuffs. It was not until chemicals became more widely used on a scientific basis in the treatment of illness that Hoffmann Laroche came on the scene in Basel in 1892. For Ciba it was a short step from the manufacture of dyestuffs to that of medicaments, and they took this step in 1892 in order to diversify their activities. In 1921 Sandoz followed suit and Geigy in 1940. When Ciba finally merged with Geigy in 1970 a vast concern was created.

Other branches of the Swiss chemical industry should be mentioned. The manufacture of perfumes and of food spices for food-processing became centred in Geneva, and this city is now a world-centre for these two fields of chemical production.

In recent years photo-chemistry and agro-chemistry have also been developed in Switzerland.

The benefits that the Swiss pharmaceutical industry has conferred on mankind are tremendous: one need only think of vitamins, sedatives and the wide spectrum of medicaments which are manufactured in Basel.

In 1979, the Swiss chemical and pharmaceutical industry employed 62,000 people in Switzerland and almost 120,000 overseas: in 1980 it accounted for one fifth of all Swiss exports.

24

The Clock and Watch-making Industry

Perhaps the best-known of Swiss industries is the clock and watch-making industry, and yet, however, few foreigners realize how vast it is.

After the book, the clock was one of the first articles to be manufactured in Switzerland: the industry developed as a direct consequence of the Reformation. In 1541, John Calvin, the Protestant reformer, settled in Geneva. He preached an ascetic life-style, and declared such golden fabrications as crosses, chalices and other precious articles, which were dear to the Roman Catholic Church, as idolatrous, and by so doing deprived the goldsmiths of Geneva of much of their livelihood. In 1554, however, a certain Thomas Bayard came to Geneva as Calvin's assistant, and he was a clock-maker. The Genevese goldsmiths welcomed Bayard with open arms as a saviour and turned their activities to clock and watch-making.

The newly-founded industry was strengthened by the arrival of many Huguenot refugees from France, and gradually it spread throughout the Jura region.

The first pocket-watches were, of course, hand-made: each worker made the whole of the watch, but then came a division of labour and certain workers specialized in certain parts. The final change to factory production only materialized after bitter struggles, and it was only made possible in 1845, when the first machines were invented which could produce absolutely identical parts and so make interchangeability possible.

Invention and innovation in the clock and watch-making industry were encouraged by societies which were founded to stimulate research, and as a result of this almost all the major discoveries in watch-making have been in Switzerland. The first quartz-watch was made here in 1967. It was thanks to this emphasis on research and to the mechanization of the industry that the Swiss clock and watch-making industry was able to lead the world in watch-making for more than a hundred years.

The success of the Swiss clock and watch-making industry can be attributed to two factors, namely the high quality of the product and also the high degree of service offered to the customer. In order to make this service possible, repair agencies had to be established overseas, and in order to train foreigners, technical colleges as well. In addition, two research laboratories have been set up in Neuchâtel which foreigners are free to attend. The success of all this can be measured by the fact that Switzerland produces more than 50,000,000 clocks, watches and works annually, and most of these are exported.

25

The Chocolate and Foodstuffs Processing Industry

The Swiss chocolate and foodstuffs processing industry evolved, once again, out of necessity. Switzerland's food resources were always scarce and had to be preserved at all costs. Milk produced in summer had to be conserved for the long winter months. This was done originally by manufacturing cheese, then much later chocolate, and later still condensed milk. When food-processing arrived preservation took on a new dimension.

François Cailler started to produce chocolate in Switzerland at Vevey in 1819, but only for medicinal purposes. Then at Serrières in 1826 a confectioner named Philippe Suchard also began to crush cocoa-beans and make chocolate from them. Other chocolate manufacturers followed: Kohler (1830), Sprüngli (1845), Klaus (1856), Tobler (1869) and Lindt (1879).

In 1866 two further businesses were also founded which were to be of great consequence to the Swiss food-processing industry, namely the Anglo-Swiss Condensed Milk Co in Cham, by the American brothers Page, and secondly the business founded in Vevey by Henri Nestlé to produce a milk farina for babies. In 1878 the Anglo-Swiss Condensed Milk Co decided to manufacture its own milk foods, and the Nestlé firm replied by diversifying into the manufacture of condensed milk. A bitter rivalry ensued which only ended when the two firms merged in 1905.

Meanwhile milk chocolate had been discovered by Daniel Peter who had started to manufacture chocolate in 1867. He manufactured plain chocolate by day and experimented with the introduction of milk into chocolate during the night: his only assistant was his wife. He finally discovered the right blend and was ready to start production in 1875. His firm prospered, and in 1904 he joined forces with Kohler and shortly afterwards the two reached a business agreement with Nestlé. When Nestlé merged with the Anglo-Swiss Condensed Milk Co a year later in 1905, the basis for the rapid development of the Nestlé firm had been laid. A hundred years after its foundation, in 1966, the Nestlé firm could boast of having no fewer than 214 factories, scattered over the five continents, and a work-force of 85,000.

26

Tourism

Another source of Swiss national income is the tourist trade. Whilst from time immemorial visitors to Switzerland have enthused over her lakes and mountains, it is only really since winter sport became popular (and this thanks largely to British initiatives) and holiday resorts have had two seasons, that this industry has truly flourished. Switzerland owes her popularity as a tourist attraction not only to her natural beauty, but also to the purity of the air, to her hospitality and security and to the central position which she occupies in the heart of Europe.

The beauties of Switzerland have been well publicized by writers and poets throughout the ages, and latterly by twenty-four publicity offices in foreign countries. In 1985, the income from tourism totalled Sfr 10.1 billion or about eight per cent of total Swiss national income. Tourism has a particular regional value in the economy of the mountain districts, where agriculture and forestry alone would not suffice to provide a modern livelihood and where depopulation would otherwise ensue.

27

Agriculture

A very serious concern of the Swiss in the defence of their country is the maintenance of food supplies in times of war: to safeguard these a maximum of food is always produced.

Switzerland is one of the smaller European countries: its area is only 41,293 sq km, and of that area one quarter is totally unproductive, a second is woodland, a third quarter mostly alpine pastureland and only the fourth quarter is truly productive land which produces a variety of crops. How to feed her population has been a perpetual problem for Switzerland throughout the ages, and this led to an early industrialization of the country. The result of this industrialization is that whereas a hundred years ago more than half the population were engaged in agriculture, today it is less than six per cent. Yet despite this the yield of agricultural produce has increased during this period. Between 1946/50 and 1983 total agricultural production increased by eighty-nine per cent. This was due to land-improvement, the rationalization of cultivated areas and, not least, to mechanization. Between 1945 and 1983 the number of four-wheeled tractors used in Swiss farming increased from 1,337 to 106,000.

The Federal State has a direct interest in agriculture. Firstly, because Article 23a of the Federal Constitution directs the Government 'to maintain the necessary stores of grain for national provision'. Secondly, because the Economic Articles and the Agricultural Law state that agricultural policy shall be such that 'in order to safeguard the interests of the whole economy, a healthy farming community and an efficient agriculture, which makes provision for the nation, shall be maintained'. It follows from this that even marginal, unprofitable areas must be kept in production, and because farmers cannot increase cultivation at a moment's notice, also it follows that the

above-mentioned directives can only be fulfilled by the granting
of huge subsidies to the Swiss farming community. As some
time ago it became evident that the giving of subsidies and
protective tariffs would not suffice to put these agricultural
policies into effect, the Federal State turned to the setting of
realistic prices which would cover cost. These agricultural
policies cost the nation a huge amount of money each year. The
higher prices must, of course, be paid by the Swiss people, and
these are the concealed impositions which are mentioned at the
end of the section on taxation. To get a true comparison with
other countries, these additional prices must be taken into
account.

28

Forestry

A quarter of the area of Switzerland is covered with woodland, thirty per cent of which is owned privately and seventy per cent publicly.

Timber is the only indigenous raw material in Switzerland which is almost sufficient for the country's needs, but how long this will continue is uncertain, because, mostly as a result of air-polution, many trees in Switzerland are diseased.

Trees are of special importance to Switzerland for several reasons. Firstly, on the mountainsides they offer protection against avalanches, landslides and soil erosion; secondly, as already mentioned, they constitute a vital Swiss raw material; and thirdly, in central Switzerland, they regulate the water supply. Finally, they protect the soil from warm winds which would otherwise dry it up.

The importance of woodland to Switzerland may be seen from the fact that there has been legislation in Switzerland to protect trees for over a hundred years.

29

The Swiss Banking System

Swiss trade and industry could not have prospered, as they have, had it not been for the close co-operation and support given to them by the Swiss banks. An example of this was shown in 1985, when eight banks joined forces to provide the Biel micro-electronics and watch-making firm, ASAUG-SSIH with a Sfr 950 million credit.

A requirement for a healthy banking system is a sound national currency because banking activity depends upon money being lent to banks which they then lend to industry, trade and private people. It is essential, therefore, that if people are to save and place their money in banks, they should have confidence in the national economy and currency. This confidence in Switzerland is created by sound economic policies pursued by the Swiss financial authorities. The Swiss currency is one of the strongest in the world, largely because it must have a forty per cent minimum gold-coverage: at the present price of gold, however, the gold-coverage greatly exceeds this figure. The confidence which the Swiss people have in the Swiss financial system may be seen from the fact that the total amount of savings-capital in 1984, contrived as a result of good house-keeping by the Swiss national economy and private households amounted to Sfr 61.2 billion or Sfr 9,415 per head of the population: this savings-capital was made up of undistributed profits, private savings, surplus on Federal state and social security accounts and depreciation amounts.

A second reason why people are prepared to invest in Switzerland, even though interest rates are low, is the policy of bank secrecy which prevails in Switzerland: a third reason is the efficiency and integrity of Swiss bankers and the sound fiscal policies which their banks pursue. If the necessary capital had not been available to Swiss trade and industry, in the right quantities and at the right time, the development of trade and industry would not have been possible to the same degree. That the required capital has been available has been largely due to the thriftiness of the Swiss people and to confidence in the Swiss banking system.

The Swiss National Bank is a special statutory public limited company within Swiss Federal Law. It is administered in co-operation with and under the supervision of the Federal political authorities in accordance with the Swiss National Bank Law. It has a share capital of Sfr 50 million: around fifty-eight per cent of the shares are owned by the cantons, cantonal banks and other public bodies and about forty-two per cent by individuals. Its main tasks, as laid down by the Federal Constitution, are to regulate the circulation of money, facilitate the clearing of payments, and pursue credit and monetary policies which are conducive to the general good of the whole country. It also determines the exchange rate of the Swiss franc and has sole authority for the issuing of bank-notes.

In 1980 there were 473 banking firms in Switzerland, of which 220 were regional or savings banks. Switzerland has more publicly owned or publicly controlled banks than any other country in the world. These include the Swiss National Bank, twenty-nine cantonal banks, and forty regional and savings banks in which the communes have a majority holding. In 1984 the Swiss banking institutions employed 98,000 people, and the aggregate of all their balance-sheet totals (Bilanzsummen) came to more than three times the Swiss Gross National Product (Swiss GNP in 1984, Sfr 226 billion). The Swiss banks are strongly established in other financial market centres abroad, and make a substantial contribution to the gross national income and national balance of payments.

Swiss bank secrecy is still an emotive subject for foreigners, but a certain amount of fire would appear to have been taken out of it by the Swiss authorities' insistence that the Swiss practice of bank secrecy does not apply to monies gained criminally.

Bank secrecy is another attitude which springs from the Swiss love of personal freedom and independence. The Swiss conception of freedom has three aspects. Firstly the freedom of the State, by which is understood the freedom of the Swiss Federal State from outside domination. Secondly freedom within the State, by which is meant the entitlement of the individual to his or her basic rights as laid down in the Federal Constitution. But there is also a third aspect, namely the freedom of the individual from the State, and it is this conception which prompted the Swiss to curtail central authority by imposing a limit on the number of civil servants permitted in the administration: it is also this conception which prompts the Swiss citizen to forbid the Federal State authorities to look at his bank account. Whether this attitude is morally defensible, I leave the reader to judge.

30

Insurance

The banking and insurance industries in Switzerland are closely connected. Like the Swiss banks, so the Swiss insurance companies make a large contribution to the national income. Like the banks too, they are international in their operations, and in 1985 they contributed Sfr 660 million in overseas earnings.

As in saving, so in insuring himself, the Swiss citizen is one of the foremost in the world. For the average Swiss family, excluding motoring, insurance claims sixteen per cent, on average, of the household expenditure, and the Federal State allocates twenty-one per cent of its total expenditure to social and kindred forms of insurance.

There are some 123 insurance companies in Switzerland, of which thirteen confine their activities solely to re-insurance, and in this specialized field they lead the world.

31

Multinational Firms

The commercial and financial standing of Switzerland is out of all proportion to the size of her territory or the number of the population, for whilst she is a dwarf in size and numbers, she is of much greater stature commercially and financially.

As has been seen from the descriptions given of the five largest Swiss manufacturing industries, the leading firms in those industries have extended their activities far beyond the frontiers of Switzerland and have become multinational companies. As a result of this the Swiss national economy has become one of the most multinational of all economies: the overseas part of her economy is greater than the domestic. In 1981 the hundred largest Swiss firms employed 500,000 people abroad. Just as in the seventeenth and eighteenth centuries small countries such as Holland and England extended their territories overseas, so Switzerland has built up a huge commercial empire abroad.

The reasons for this are firstly that Switzerland is so small, her domestic commercial base so tiny, that had she not extended beyond her own frontiers, her home market would soon have been swamped by her foreign competitors, nor would she have been able to supply the finance required for research in this modern age. If Swiss firms did not have strong international positions to give them the necessary technological and financial strength, they would go under. Research today costs so much that it can only be sustained if the cost is shared internationally.

Secondly a small country is compelled to produce abroad if her domestic supplies of raw materials and manpower are in short supply, and especially so if she has no direct access to the sea.

Finally many countries close their frontiers to foreign imports and compel the multinationals to set up factories within their own borders. This is because these developing countries need the commercial expertise of countries like Switzerland in order to develop their own natural resources, and so create jobs for their own people.

The advantages for these Swiss multinational companies from operating abroad are that they can offer Swiss products worldwide, in that these foreign branches can also be used as bases for export to other foreign countries. This would not be possible without an international framework. Moreover the experience gained from this worldwide framework is of immense value to these firms.

So Switzerland now has a vast commercial empire which is controlled and managed from the home base in Switzerland, and this commercial empire makes a considerable contribution to the Swiss national economy.

32

Research

In describing those large Swiss industries which have gradually become multinational concerns stress has been laid on the need for research. For the Swiss economy research on a large scale is vital in order to ensure that her scanty natural resources and manpower are used to the best advantage. Switzerland can only keep ahead of her competitors by perfecting present products and discovering new ones. For this Switzerland is dependent on the expertise and experience of her workers and on years of research.

The Swiss are very sensitive to the fact that to keep ahead of their industrial competitors much money must be spent on research, and therefore all large Swiss industries pour large sums into it. The Swiss chemical and pharmaceutical industry is a good example, for to keep this industry going vast sums of money are needed because research is so costly: research in the Swiss chemical and pharmaceutical industry costs around Sfr 7 million a working day. This is not surprising when one realizes that around 10,000 chemical compositions must be built up, either by synthesis or from natural organisms, before one is found which proves itself as suitable for a new medicament. The chemical and pharmaceutical industry, therefore, has to employ many qualified people: twelve per cent of all employees in this industry have university degrees or their equivalent. The financing of this industry would be impossible without the backing of the Swiss banking system.

In 1975, per head of the population, the Swiss spent more on research than any other country in the world: almost twenty per cent more than was spent by America, and again, per head of the population, Swiss private industry spent more than three times as much in that year on research as was spent by private firms in Britain. Almost two thirds of the cost of research in Switzerland is borne by industry itself. The largest Swiss firms have extensive research laboratories, both in Switzerland and abroad, and others are provided by the Swiss educational institutions. It is estimated that of the total monies spent by Swiss universities, between twenty-five per cent and forty-five per cent goes on research and development. It is only by investing a part of her income in research that Switzerland is able to keep ahead of her international competitors.

33

Patents

Research is safeguarded by the patenting system. A patent confers on the possessor of some new discovery the right to forbid others to use or copy it for a defined period (twenty years in Switzerland). If the owner does not wish to make use of the new discovery himself, he can sell his invention to a third person or allow others to use it on licence, for which he will receive a small percentage of the proceeds from sales which stem from his discovery. This again is a good source of income for Switzerland, because in Switzerland, in proportion to the population, more patents are registered than in any other country.

Patenting stimulates invention because it safeguards the benefit which accrues from a discovery to the inventor himself. As already mentioned, the trade in patents and licences to manufacture inventions is a highly profitable business for Switzerland and contributes to her exports.

Switzerland's industrial success is due, in a large measure, to research and the discoveries and new technology which have ensued from it. In Swiss trade and industry the emphasis is on quality, prompt delivery and a compliance with the customer's special requirements: made to measure is the order of the day.

34

Trading Companies

In addition to the large Swiss multinational firms already mentioned, there are also very big Swiss trading companies involved in overseas trade. They do not seek publicity and their names would probably mean little to the man-in-the-street. They were mostly founded in the latter half of the last century for the promotion of the sale of Swiss goods overseas, but as they grew they built factories abroad and diversified into trading in commodities of all kinds. Today their activities are multifarious and worldwide, and they contribute tremendously to Swiss overseas trade.

35

Railways

Swiss industry and commerce could not have flourished without an adequate system of communications, both within and with the outside world.

As we have seen, Switzerland's economic importance is partly due to the fact that she lies at the crossroads of Europe. The original forms of transport on these transit routes were the mule in the mountains and the boat across the lakes. With the construction of better roads across the Alps, however, the horse-drawn vehicle took over from the mule-pack: but the real break through in communications did not come until railways were built.

The story of the construction of the Swiss railways is a saga in itself. The first railway on Swiss soil was opened in 1844: it connected Strasbourg with Basel. The first Swiss railway as such followed three years later and ran from Zurich to Baden. From these beginnings the network was gradually extended to cover the whole of the country. To accomplish this, colossal feats of constructional engineering were required: one need only think of the Gotthard Tunnel and its approaches, or of the construction of the railway up the Jungfrau to the highest railway station in the world.

The organization and running of the Swiss railways is as impressive as their construction. The difficulties which the weather presents to efficient time-keeping in winter are considerable, and yet delays on the Swiss Federal Railways, even in winter, are the exception rather than the rule.

For some time now the new Swiss Railways' timetable has been in operation, by which inter-city trains connect the main Swiss towns and cities at regular hourly intervals, leaving at the same time each hour from the same platform: this is to be extended.

These main line trains have connections with international trains, trains on branch lines, mountain railways and post autobuses, as well as with certain boats on the lakes. In 1980 a railway was built to Zurich airport and in 1987 to Geneva airport also, so that there are now direct connections with air flights as well.

Many of these railway services are run at a loss, but as the railway network is regarded as being part of the defence system and also a public service, the railways are heavily subsidized by the Federal State.

Traffic on certain routes of Swiss Railways is so dense (250 trains a day through the Gotthard Tunnel for example) that new lines will have to be built. To this end the 'Rail 2000' project has been drawn up, whereby new tracks will be constructed across Switzerland to accommodate high-speed trains and so provide high-speed connections with the countries bordering on Switzerland.

Nor should the Swiss cable-car network be forgotten which gives tourists access to the mountain tops.

In the field of transport it should not be overlooked, either, that Switzerland has her own airline, Swissair, which with its 18,000 employees is one of the largest airlines in the world. In 1986 Swissair machines flew 108.4 million kilometres.

For Switzerland, transport by water has three aspects. Firstly there are the boats on the lakes, now mostly diesel-driven, but with the old paddle-steamers becoming ever more popular as a tourist attraction. Then there is the river Rhine, which offers Switzerland the only direct water-connection with the sea for shipping. Shipping on the Rhine is especially adapted to the conveyance of heavy goods, and in consequence of this the Basel Rhine harbours play an important role in the importing of heavy goods into Switzerland. Finally Switzerland's high seas merchant fleet should not be forgotten: it consists of twenty-nine merchantmen with a carrying capacity of around half-a-million tons.

36

Swiss Democracy

Switzerland is a semi-direct democracy: it is semi-direct because in certain instances political decisions are taken directly by the people, as for example, at the Landsgemeinde (public assembly) or in referenda, but in others they are taken indirectly by representatives chosen by them, as for example, in the various parliaments. But even in the election of representatives, responsible methods are used.

Switzerland uses two different voting methods in choosing her representatives: the first is the majority system and the second the proportional representation method. If the majority system is employed, then dependent upon which type of majority is used, an absolute majority or a relative majority, that candidate is elected who either secures an overall majority of votes cast (fifty per cent plus one) in the first case, or the largest number of votes cast in the second. The States Council which represents the cantons, and most cantonal governments, are elected mainly by the majority system, but the National Council, representing the people, is chosen by the proportional representation method.

The majority system is straightforward. In each canton the political parties adopt the same number of candidates as there are seats available, and in the voting which follows, in the first vote a candidate is usually required to obtain an absolute majority of votes cast to be elected. In subsequent votes, if these prove necessary, it is usually only required of a candidate that he or she should obtain the most votes cast to be elected.

In the election of the larger chamber, the National Council, it has been deemed fairer that it should be elected by the proportional representation method. In this system of election each party compiles a list of candidates according to the number of seats available, and these are submitted to the voter together with a blank list. The voter has great freedom of choice. He can adopt the complete list of the party he favours, or, if he disapproves of certain candidates on that list, he can delete their names and replace them with names from other lists. If he especially approves of a candidate he can double up, in other words delete one name from the list and give his favoured candidate two votes. He can even compile his own list on the blank form using the names of any of the valid candidates on any of the lists. Seats are then allocated to the parties in proportion to the votes cast for them.

The advantage of this proportional representation election system is that no vote is lost: each vote counts, both to the candidate and to his party. The fact that each voter knows that his vote is of significance gives him a greater sense of political importance, an awareness of his sovereignty.

The Swiss equip themselves for responsible decision making in political affairs by listening on radio and television to news bulletins, reports on Parliament and current affairs programmes, much of which transmission is devoted to domestic topics and by reading one or more of the Swiss newspapers which publish 3.45 million copies daily. Research has shown that between eighty per cent and ninety per cent of Swiss male youth are readers of a serious Swiss newspaper.

37

The Swiss People

So far in answer to the question posed by the title of this book, 'What Makes Switzerland Tick?' we have only cited the mechanism, the political, social and commercial framework within which the Swiss people 'live and move and have their being': to this must be added that force which drives the mechanism, namely the Swiss people themselves, because in Switzerland, as perhaps in no other country, the people are 'sovereign' or 'boss'.

The word 'sovereign' in the English-speaking world usually means a ruler or monarch, but in Switzerland it means quite simply 'the people'. This sovereignty is ensured to enfranchised Swiss citizens by the Federal Constitution, because this confers the right of initiative and referendum on them and by so doing invests sovereign authority in them. The Federal Constitution states that all acts of Federal legislation must be directly or tacitly endorsed by the people and cantons before they can become law.

Where the referendum is compulsory, it is called an 'Obligatory Referendum', and this type of referendum applies before a total revision of the Federal Constitution or the introduction of any Federal law or decree which would permanently change the Federal Constitution, can become law. It is also required before the entry into any international collective security organization, such as NATO, or to a supranational society, such as UNO.

The 'Facultative Referendum' (Optional Referendum) applies to other Federal laws and decrees where no amendment to the Federal Constitution is involved, and before the entering into of certain international treaties. After a law has been passed by Parliament, the facultative referendum leaves the enfranchised citizens free, if they wish, to demand a referendum on that law, providing they can obtain 50,000 signatures of valid voters, within ninety days to their request otherwise the measure automatically becomes law: eight cantons may do the same.

The right of initiative gives the enfranchised citizens the opportunity to initiate legislation themselves for a partial or total revision of the Federal Constitution: they must obtain 100,000 valid signatures to their request within eighteen months. The initiative can be in the form of a fully worked-out measure or merely a proposal to the Federal Council to enact something. The cantons have similar rights. An initiative must be authenticated by the commune authorities where it originates. The Federal Council is compelled to respond to a valid initiative from the people or cantons by submitting it to a referendum of people and cantons. So the enfranchised Swiss citizens are doubly sovereign in that they can initiate legislation by means of the initiative and they can nullify it by means of the referendum: this applies at both national and cantonal level. By their election of representatives to the Federal and cantonal parliaments they can also, indirectly, exert influence on the course of legislation.

Sovereignty, however, carries with it responsibility and this is, perhaps, the secret of the success of the Swiss people in the political and social fields, namely that they are willing to accept responsibility for the well-being of their country and that they are well-fitted to exercise it. They do not expect a professional standing-army to defend them, but accept the fact that they must defend themselves and that the defence of their fatherland begins at their own front door, using the rifles and ammunition which they keep at home permanently. They do not look to the Federal State to provide for them but would rather stand each on his own legs and keep the Federal State at arm's length.

Personal responsibility, of course, always incorporates civic responsibility: duty to one's neighbour. The Swiss are very alive to this fact, and within the framework of the militia system, which they have extended to parts of the national, cantonal and communal administration, the individual is able to offer his contribution to the common good. A Swiss male, in his capacity as militia man, gives a year of his life to the defence of his country: between twenty and fifty years of age he serves 365 days, an Army officer much more. At the same time, when not on active service, he may participate in either local government administration, civil defence, the fire service, school commune or religious commune or committees of enquiry, not to mention his activities as member of a political party or trade union or some professional association, and all this is usually done in a voluntary or semi-voluntary capacity.

The average Swiss is closest to communal life, that is to that of the village or community in which he lives. In a political commune there are many functions to be fulfilled, because the commune is the lowest rung of the administrative ladder and therefore has to execute federal, cantonal and communal decrees. The implication would be from this that a whole host of civil servants would be required to do the administrative work of the commune, but this is not so. Such is the response from the people to offer themselves to perform community tasks, that many small communes have no salaried full-time official at all. Only when the commune becomes a certain size do we find two full-time officials, the commune secretary and the commune accountant. Larger communes, naturally, have more, but they are always kept to a minimum. Most of the other tasks would appear to be carried out militia-wise. Many would say that it would be impossible to have an efficient, well-organized local administration in this way. This is not true: very often the expertise available from volunteers in the community is greater than that which would be offered by full-time civil servants.

The militia system holds good, not only for local administration and local political and social life, but also for the parliaments, both national and cantonal, for the district courts and for many cantonal courts. There are very few Swiss who at some time have not occupied some office in commune administration or in a political body, trade union, employers' association, club, society or in some community work, be it only as members of some committee or commission. Every Swiss understands that he or she is expected to be responsible for something, and to participate in one way or another in community work. In this an example is set from the very top of the political structure. The Federal President is president for one year only and then will revert back to being an ordinary member of the Cabinet. When he retires he will receive no knighthood or peerage but will merely retain his honoured title of 'Alt-Bundesrat', and will probably be expected to put the political experience which he has gleaned throughout his political life at the disposal of his local commune.

This part-time involvement in political and social affairs on the part of the average citizen means that the country can be administered at a minimum of expense, and therefore taxes can be kept low. It also means that the person involved should become more fully aware of the problems of administration, and by co-operating with his fellows to solve those problems should also become more practical, more responsible and more understanding. From this direct involvement with others in public affairs stems tolerance and that readiness on the part of the Swiss to co-operate and compromise. Because the Swiss are practical people, they prefer small political and social units which are controllable and manageable, hence their penchant for federalism rather than for a huge centralized state. Federalism also enables them to give a fair hearing and say in affairs to minority groups, and in a country such as Switzerland, composed of people from such diverse backgrounds, speaking four different languages and almost equally divided between two different religious confessions, this is essential.

The Swiss are proud of their country and rightly so. Very many are consequently willing to make sacrifices for it. Above all they are proud of the fairness of their political institutions and of their society. The foundations for this fairness are laid in school, where children from all backgrounds meet on equal terms and the highest forms of education are open to every child: a Swiss child knows from the outset that success in life depends on his or her efforts. This is also true later of army life where promotion is based on competency, and where a person from a less fortunate background may command those from a more fortunate background.

A Swiss person during his or her life plays many roles in the political, social and vocational life of the country. Sometimes they are at the helm, at others they serve before the mast, but the fact that they accept a position of authority in any one of these capacities means that they should adopt a responsible attitude in all the others.

The responsibility shown by the Swiss as individuals is also reflected at national level, in the past and present, as is shown by the apportioning of total national expenditure (Federal State, cantons and communes) in 1983.

Responsible attitudes adopted in the past contributed to the fact that in 1983 only 6.8 per cent of total national expenditure had to be spent on finance expenses and interest payments on national indebtedness. Against this 19.6 per cent was spent on educating the next generation and on research to help to ensure jobs for them. Thanks to the militia system of part-time political and social commitment to running the country on the part of the people, only 6.4 per cent of the annual national budget had to be spent on administration. Thanks also to the responsible attitudes of individual citizens in accepting a large degree of personal responsibility for ensuring against the vagaries of life, only 14.3 per cent needed to be spent on social welfare and 11.4 per cent on health services.

The Swiss national expense allocations (Federal State, cantons and communes) for the year 1983 were as follows:

Education and research	19.6 per cent
Social welfare	14.3 per cent
Transport and energy	11.8 per cent
Health services	11.4 per cent
Defence	8.3 per cent
Finance expenses and interest payments	6.8 per cent
Administration	6.4 per cent
Environment	4.0 per cent
Agriculture and food	3.7 per cent
Culture, recreation, sport	3.0 per cent
Miscellaneous	10.7 per cent
	100.0 per cent

The tendency of the Swiss to look to the future is also discernible in Swiss educational policy, in that in Switzerland, proportionally, more children are given a commercial or industrial vocational training than in most industrial countries. This means that in future, as now, a very large percentage of Swiss people will be involved in directly creating the wherewithal to live: that is in producing marketable products of one sort or another directly. Against this the number of civil servants involved in Federal State, cantonal and communal administration has been kept to a minimum, and is small by international standards.

Responsibility has also been shown by the Federal State in respect of national defence: here, in this atomic age, the emphasis is on survival. It is realized that the discovery of the atom bomb has brought with it a new defence dimension: it is no longer a question of merely defending the terrain of the country, but also the population. As to the defence of the terrain by the Army, all that need be said is that Switzerland is, perhaps, one of the easier countries of the world to defend, thanks to its mountainous character, and that as regards conventional weapons, perhaps one of the better defended.

38

Switzerland

A Classless Society?

Spectacular as has been Switzerland's 'economic miracle' and rapid rise to prosperity, her social achievements have also been impressive, for I believe that the Swiss, since 1848, have accomplished, to a great extent, what the French Revolutionaries aimed at, and later Socialists and Communists set out to achieve and often very largely failed: namely of having established, to a large degree, a socially classless society, and this within the context of one of the most capitalistic countries in the world.

This is perhaps best exemplified by the experience of a friend of mine who travels widely. She told me that not long ago she took a taxi in a Communist country to the airport. They arrived an hour early and my friend invited the taxi-driver to have a meal with her at the airport restaurant. He flatly refused because such are the social distinctions in that Communist country that only the Communist hierarchy are permitted to use such restaurants, and so she had to give him money for his meal in the canteen and she made her way to the airport restaurant alone. In contrast to this, in Switzerland, where she regularly takes a taxi from her home to Geneva airport, the local taxi-driver invariably has a meal with her in the airport restaurant if they arrive early for a plane. It would appear that in Communist countries class distinction and privilege have not been abolished, but merely transferred from the old privileged classes to the new political hierarchy.

If the impression given by this book so far is that Switzerland possesses a perfect democratic and social system, then that impression is, of course, false. There are flaws and shortcomings in Swiss democracy, just as there are in every human institution.

One danger to the continued implementation and development of democracy in Switzerland would appear to be a certain political apathy on the part of many Swiss citizens: the degree of participation at elections and referenda very often leaves much to be desired. Whether this political indifference on the part of many Swiss people stems from complacency or from satisfaction with the present state of affairs in Switzerland would appear to be an open question. Another doubt being expressed in Switzerland is whether today community spirit is as pronounced as it was previously, or whether newly-found affluence is not breeding increased indifference, on the part of some Swiss people, towards community obligations.

There is also the danger that too strong an insistence on conformity and duty can become personally oppressive, inhibiting, and in the end counterproductive. A further criticism heard in Switzerland is that as a result of an accumulation of roles by certain individuals, the management of Swiss political and economic affairs is in too few hands. If this is true and proves to be detrimental to the country, once again the remedy lies in the hands of the 'sovereign' people.

Swiss political thinkers would appear to be fully aware of the failings and hidden dangers in Swiss democracy. Erich Kägi in his book 'Demokratie durchleuchtet' (Democracy Examined) reflects very deeply on democracy in Switzerland. Hans Tschäni, in his two books, 'Wer regiert die Schweiz?' (Who rules Switzerland?) and 'Wem gehört die Schweiz?' (Who owns Switzerland?) examines the political and social structures of the country very thoroughly. So long as this vigilance persists, efforts are likely to be made to counter whatever political and social defects exist now or may appear in the future in Swiss life.

But Switzerland is a small country, and as a result of her political make-up and tradition, especially that of federalism, she would appear to have a greater opportunity than many countries to innovate and experiment in the political field and thereby to be in a position to implement democracy more effectively.

So the answer to the question posed by the title of this booklet must be: first, that Switzerland would appear to have succeeded in creating a political, social and judicial framework which is reasonably fair and just. A framework adapted to the needs, aspirations and outlook of her people: one within which her trade and industry can flourish. A framework which encourages the individual to work, save and give of himself to his fellows, which stimulates personal effort by offering opportunity to all and by rewarding justly when that effort is made. A framework in which the individual has a wealth of personal freedom and human rights.

But this is only half the answer to the question: the other half is, quite simply, the Swiss people themselves. Over the centuries of Swiss history the people have developed into instruments fitted to operate such a political, social and economic system effectively. It may have been the sparseness of Switzerland's natural resources which prompted them to become a nation of practical commonsense traders, or it may have been the hazards of the mountains which taught them foresight: a miscalculation in predicting the weather in the mountains can be fatal. What we do know is that over the years they have developed into a freedom-loving, independent, responsible people, whose propensity for hard work and qualities of thrift, commonsense and foresight have enabled them to fit into a political, social and economic framework which they have created, and to operate extremely efficiently within it. The result is clear to see − a Switzerland which is one of the most stable, law-abiding and prosperous countries in the world.

The question remains, 'Is this Swiss political and social system exportable to other countries?' I think the honest answer to that question must be 'In its entirety, no!' because the backgrounds of other countries are quite different. But what I think can be confidently asserted is that the various components which make up the Swiss success story, namely federalism, the militia system, the division of competencies and the emphasis on small units, could, perhaps, be of benefit severally and in varying degrees to other countries. Nor is there any doubt that the attitude to life which is inculcated into a Swiss person from the cradle to the grave and which is largely responsible for any success which the Swiss may have had, namely personal responsibility, is valid everywhere.

To a foreigner living in Switzerland, the impression left of the Swiss people and their country is one of moderation, tolerance and compromise and it is these which create the right climate for the solving of Swiss problems. They stem from a balanced attitude and outlook which the Swiss possess to a large degree.

In politics this balance can be seen in the fact that the two houses of Parliament are of equal standing, yet elected largely by different electoral systems. The full cantons, though differing in size, have equal status in the States Council. In the allocation of competencies between the Federal State, cantons and communes, a balance has to be kept. The Federal State allocates subsidies equitably between the cantons. The three main languages used are regarded as being equal, as are the main religious confessions. In industry the two sides, employers and employees, are regarded as being of equal standing. Many more examples of balance in Swiss life could be given. Fanatics and rigid doctrinaires would appear to be anathema to the Swiss, because they are practical people who throughout their history have learned to come to terms with their fellows and to co-operate with them.

Nor would the writer of this booklet himself wish to appear dogmatic, from the portrayal of Switzerland that he has given here. The purpose in writing the booklet has been to try to discover the forces which motivate the Swiss and the outcome of that motivation, in the hope that by so doing, others, more competent than he, might look critically at this Swiss experience and glean any lessons from it that it might have to offer. And if by so doing, other countries with similar problems to the Swiss were able to be helped, then the purpose in writing the booklet would have been doubly fulfilled.